SMART ACTORS, FOOLISH CHOICES

KATHERINE MAYFIELD

SMART ACTORS, FOOLISH CHOICES

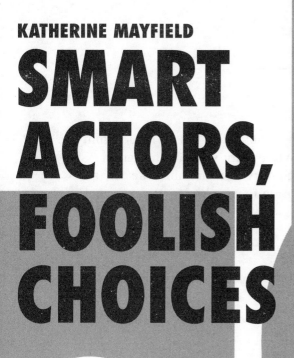

A SELF-HELP GUIDE
TO COPING WITH THE
EMOTIONAL STRESSES
OF THE BUSINESS

BACK STAGE BOOKS

An imprint of Watson-Guptill Publications, New York

Katherine Mayfield has been performing for over twenty years in theaters across the country, and in film, theater, and television in New York City.

First published in 1996 in the United States by Back Stage Books, an imprint of Watson-Guptill Publications, a division of BPI Communications, Inc., 1515 Broadway, New York, NY 10036-8986.

Library of Congress Cataloging-in-Publication Data for this title can be obtained by writing to the Library of Congress, Washington, DC.

Manufactured in the United States of America

ISBN 0-8230-8424-8

Senior Editor: Paul Lukas

Associate Editor: Dale Ramsey

Designer: Jay Anning

Production Manager: Ellen Greene

1 2 3 4 5 / 00 99 98 97 96

To Alan Langdon,
who started me on the road to finding myself;

to Tamar Shapiro,
who showed me the way;

and to my parents,
who encouraged me throughout the process.

ACKNOWLEDGMENTS

Thanks to all who showed interest in the theme of this book and encouraged me throughout the process of writing it: To Anne V. Sawyer, for her unflagging support and validation; to Tamar Shapiro, for her life-giving attention and help; to Emily T., for getting me started and for her enthusiasm and spirit; to Jerry Fargo and Roberta Rohdin of the "For Performers" support group, whose wonderful and important work with actors first sparked the idea for the book; to Annette Lieberman, for her excellent guidance and encouragement of actors in the Money Awareness Program^{SM} at The Actor's Fund; to all the people who work through The Actor's Fund to give guidance and support to actors; to all the actors who graciously gave their time and shared their thoughts and feelings in the interviews; to Jim Brodsky, for his help in filling in the gaps in the book; to my parents, for their love and encouragement; to my agent, Susan Schorr, for her knowledgable advice; to Dale Ramsey, for clarifying my thoughts and helping me to uncover the truth; to Jay Anning, who gave the book its striking design; and to my editor, Paul Lukas, who believed in the project from the beginning, who answered my innumerable questions with infinite patience, and without whose gentle encouragement and wise advice the book would have fallen through the cracks in my life.

CONTENTS

FOREWORD

I once had an actor refuse to leave my office until I gave him a job. He confronted me with the accusation that I had blacklisted him and kept him from getting hired. This was a frightening moment for both of us— for me because I didn't know if he was going to physically attack me; for him because he was desperate and irrational, and believed that Mari Lyn Henry, director of casting for ABC, personified all his difficulties in the business. It was too late then for him to repair the damage to his psyche, but I think if he could have read this book some time earlier he would have benefitted from it. Practicing author Katherine Mayfield's exercises to release frustration and negativity would have helped him get in touch with why he had wanted to be an actor in the first place.

Unfortunately, actors have never had it easy, and, until very recently, books have scarcely been available to give them support. Back before the unions were established to ensure a better way of life for professionals, things were even worse. Actors encountered filthy backstage conditions and worked long hours for poverty wages. Greedy managers stole receipts and left unpaid performers stranded. Many actors ended their days without savings, pensions, or property. Complaining about the conditions in New York in 1842, one actor wrote in a letter to a colleague in England: "I hope the state of things here is sufficiently known in England to prevent any more victims being seduced by scheming rascals to come out here to starve. . . . The truth is seen by stock actors who have been here all their lives. None of them have a dollar, all are poor."

Yet, in spite of their misfortunes and many negative attitudes towards them, actors demonstrated the grit to survive. Impassioned by the roar of the crowd, the smell of the greasepaint, the name gleaming on the marquee, the "rush" that occurs on opening night, or simply a devotion to their craft, they endured. They organized themselves and overcame much adversity. They had that burning need to act that was beautifully articulated by Clara Morris: "If, without noticing the quality or length of your part, the plain fact of acting something thrills you with nameless joy . . . your fate is sealed. Nature cries to you through your brain, heart, and nerve. *Act You Must!*

Before I became a casting director, I myself had known since my fifth-grade teacher cast me in the school play that I wanted to be an actress. I don't remember the content of that play—only the fun I had wearing my mother's clothes and wobbling in her high heels. At the end of the school term I received the best actor medal for my professionalism, apparently for not peeking through the curtains to wave to my parents. To this day I regret that I wasn't living in New York or Los Angeles where there were professional training programs for young people and work opportunities in television, radio, and film as well as on the stage. So I took advantage of every opportunity to perform, reciting history passages or poetry in grammar school, taking part in school plays and forensics, and ultimately finding acceptance and support by majoring in speech and drama in college.

Finally, I went into the graduate program in theater at Catholic University of America and the late Father Gilbert V. Hartke, founder of the department, cast me as the young Miss Dove opposite Helen Hayes in *Good Morning, Miss Dove*. I was in awe of her, the First Lady of the American Theater, who taught me the importance of understanding the human heart, of trusting your instincts, of integrity, and of the true meaning of grace under pressure. And she encouraged me to continue acting.

Years later, when I was casting commercials, I would visit Miss Hayes backstage or chat with her at a social gathering. When she would ask what I was doing, I felt that my response was a disappointment. I realized, though, that if I had continued acting after completing my master's degree, I would never have known the joy and satisfaction of casting actors in roles that helped them keep the wolf from the door and to know enough financial security to pursue stage work. I had needed to gain control of my life, and I knew that actors, unless they make it big, don't have that kind of control. Many of my colleagues who are talent agents, casting directors, producers, directors, playwrights, and teachers had also begun as actors and had realized that they, too, needed more authority, respect, and power over rejection. We had acknowledged that we needed a more secure profession.

As early as 1903, Clara Morris was advising young women who considered a career on the stage: "Would-be actresses can see that their own numbers constitute one of the greatest obstacles in their path. There is also the number of trained actresses who are out of engagements. There is probably no profession in the world so overcrowded as is the profession of acting."

The statistics are still appalling. With so many union members and so few jobs, competition is fierce. Open calls posted in *Back Stage* or on union bulletin boards attract hordes of hopefuls who line up on the street hours before the sessions begin. Not long ago, when a noted film director had an open call on a bitterly cold February day, an estimated 5,000 actors (some of whom had slept on the street the night before) turned out for that big break. I once supervised an open call for a contract role on the soap opera *General Hospital*, and between 10 AM and 6 PM, more than a thousand women passed through the revolving doors. Most of them "typed out." Nevertheless, actors will never be dissuaded from trying their luck in the Big Apple or seeking their glory in Tinseltown.

Thus *Smart Actors, Foolish Choices* came to be written as a guide just for them. According to its author, the book is designed to help the actor understand the relationship between the art and the business of acting. Many actors are ignorant about the business aspect of the profession. It may seem romantic in the opera *La Bohème* to live in a cold garret, sacrificing everything for art. But there is really no excuse for seeking a career in acting without having enough money saved to survive during one's orientation. Actors should consider themselves entrepreneurs, self-appointed commanders of their own *Enterprise*. They should know how to package themselves, promote their talents, arrange their appointments, behave appropriately in interviews and on the phone, keep a daily journal of their experiences, continue training to keep in physical, mental, and emotional shape, remain open to the unexpected occurrences in the business, and develop increasing self-awareness.

Actors must make a living. When they are desperate for money, that hunger interferes with the quality of their interviews and auditions. Having a survival job in a show business–related industry is healthier for actors than working in a rigid and noncreative environment. I've known smart actors who have made the foolish choice to work at jobs that interfered with their goal of pursuing acting eight hours a day. I have also known performers who work for a famous catering concern whose actor-friendly boss knows that they have to take time off for auditions and acting engagements. This employer, meanwhile, likes and benefits from their discipline, hard work, and good people skills. Then there is the home-office solution: With so many large corporations downsizing, there are opportunities to work at home on a computer and maintain flexible hours.

Actors need to understand their own power. Why do so many fear agents and casting directors? Those people represent *power*. Just as I was once in awe of Helen Hayes, actors have been in awe of or intimidated by me—not me the person but me the holder of a position or title. I always tried to make the actor feel comfortable in the interview because I wanted to see the sense of self that empowers the person. In the audition that same sense of self enriches the quality of the work. Relaxation is important in achieving the most spontaneous and creative interpretation of a character. When actors are uncomfortable, nervous, frightened, they cannot produce a satisfactory reading because their creative energies are blocked.

There are people in power who abuse their privileges. They are, fortunately, in the minority. I have been present at auditions where the producers never looked up from the résumés before them, shuffled papers, or smoked a cigar. I've even seen one taking phone calls *during* the audition! I have heard some of my colleagues take sadistic pleasure in dissecting a performer's physical packaging or dismissing an actor abruptly. I have heard stories of actors being yelled at for no apparent reason. There are a number of dysfunctional people who have been attracted to this industry and wound up in powerful positions.

You are never going to be loved by everyone you meet. But if you give permission for others to humiliate you, they will. *Smart Actors, Foolish Choices* summons actors to regain self-esteem, overcome the fear of rejection, and enjoy a relationship with their inner child. Convinced that the way an actor relates to the business is influenced by experiences that occurred in childhood and adolescence, Katherine Mayfield shows how to turn around the negativity relating to your self and the business, resulting in greater control over your emotions and an ability to take charge of your career. And she reminds her audience that not everyone in the business wishes to deliberately mistreat actors. The smart actor will recognize the difference between user–abusers and professionals who understand both the art of the actor and the erratic nature of the business and can show their empathy.

If acting is your only reality, if you don't feel validated unless you are working, if being between engagements is endangering your quality of life, if personal relationships are strained, if it isn't fun anymore, then perhaps it is time to reassess your options. Take time off. I have known burnt-out professionals who needed time to raise children, get an extra degree, change career paths, or find another creative outlet. I have seen them return to the boards enriched by life experience and feeling less insecure, more in control of who they are.

Oscar-winning actor Anthony Hopkins, in a interview, revealed that he went through a personal and emotional crisis in the mid-1970s: "I sort of reached my wits' end," he said. "I saw that my life was running downhill . . . so I started a whole new series of habits. When I made that conscious decision to change direction . . . my life took on a whole new color and hue of brightness and has been blessed ever since." He also believes an actor must have a personal life: "Acting used to consume my existence. Now it's my job."

The content of this book is predicated on three unchangeable facts. One, there will always be actors seeking opportunities to share their talents; two, they will always need to remember that success will only happen if they treat the profession as a business; and three, they should have a support system of family, friends, and peer groups, which is essential for personal well-being.

And they need to value and affirm themselves, for the road to success is strewn with frustration, nay-sayers, sacrifice, and feelings of failure. Another Oscar winner, Mercedes Reuhl, has spoken of the times in her early career when she was uncertain within herself how much talent she had. "I believed in myself fiercely when I was receiving encouragement from Uta Hagen and felt I was proceeding gracefully," she recalled. But then the weather would change and she would allow herself to doubt herself: "These ill winds of rejection have thrown me way off course." One of the times she let that happen she started packing her bags to quit New York and the actor's life and return home. It was then that an eleventh-hour call came from a playwright who wanted her for a role. The rest is history.

Mari Lyn Henry

INTRODUCTION

This is a book for the heart and soul of the actor—for the human being behind the artist. It's not a book on acting technique, and it's not a "nuts and bolts of the business" book. It's about learning to grow, about clearing away pain and negativity that are connected to your past so that you can find joy and satisfaction in your life, and about finding ways to fulfill your potential.

The goal of this book is to help you be successful, both as a person and as an actor. It aims to help you remove major obstacles on your path to success by understanding and working through emotional issues that are buried in your past. If you are new to the business, the ideas presented in this book can help you free yourself from emotional issues before they have a chance to cause problems in your relationships with producers, agents, and others in the performing arts. If you are a veteran actor, you may resolve stumbling blocks you have encountered time after time in your pursuit of an acting career.

Discovering where you're "coming from" and how you approach the business can make all the difference between success and failure in your acting career.

A career in acting can appear to be a way to satisfy emotional needs that were neglected when you were a child—a need for attention from others, a need to express yourself, or a need for respect. A number of actors may have unconciously chosen this particular career (especially in New York, Los Angeles, or other major cities) because the structure of the business and the difficulties involved can actually mirror problematic situations from their childhood and/or adolescence. Yet it's extremely unlikely that an actor will be able to get his or her emotional needs met in the business, and very few who try to do so succeed. But once you discover how your past colors your individual perceptions, it will get easier for you to find your own ways of approaching the business, and you'll find other ways to satisfy your needs, rather than depending on the business and your career to get what you want.

If you have never examined your feelings and beliefs in the light of your adult life, you may be relating to people or situations based on emotions and perceptions that arise from the past: from your relationships with family members, your responses to parents or teachers, or your early interactions with your peers. Individual perceptions of certain situations and people are often emotionally colored by experiences from childhood. When children are young, they develop a view of the world based on the family and the environment in which they grow up. When they become adults, they will usually continue living their lives on the basis of the perceptions and beliefs they developed in childhood without creating a new emotional "map" of the world to fit their adult lives. All families are imperfect in one way or another, and most have serious problems which cause children to create maps that are distorted and unrealistic. They then continue to follow these maps as adults because the maps worked in the past, and because they know no other way.

Familiar feelings and perceptions from childhood can be activated automatically by present situations and give rise to specific patterns of behavior. Even a particular phrase or tone of voice can trigger unconcious response patterns from the past. If such patterns are not uncovered and understood, you may experience difficult emotional episodes—of fear or depression, for instance—relating to your career. Many patterns of behavior can also affect the way others in the business perceive you, sometimes in a negative way.

Think for a moment about the relationship between acting, the thing you love to do that seems to encompass and feed your very soul, and the business, which most actors grumble and grouch about and attend to grudgingly. Does this relationship remind you of (for instance) a situation from your past in which you were excited to the core of your being but felt a need to prove yourself, or in which you wanted, with a child's neediness, for those "in power" to accept, acknowledge, and delight in who you are? Many facets of the acting business as it is today may reflect your past experiences in this way. Issues from the past can be difficult to deal with, but it's necessary to confront them in order be more successful and to deal with the business in a less emotionally charged and more realistic way.

The first part of *Smart Actors, Foolish Choices* offers theories and suggestions as to where obstacles may arise for you as you build your career, as well as questions you can ask yourself which will help you begin to explore the emotional issues that can cause you confusion in your own life and career. The second half of the book offers insights into problems that can come up along the way, through interviews with twelve actors who have spent a number of years pursuing the business and gaining insight into some of the problems that actors face. In the Appendix, "Exercises to Build Self-Esteem," you will find some helpful approaches to uncovering and resolving the kinds of emotional issues that result in misdirection and unwise career choices, which lead you down false roads and hold you back from success.

It is not my contention that *every* actor has these types of emotional issues; the ideas and suggestions are offered here only for any individual who chooses to consider them. The ideas presented in this book are intended only as a guide. Because each individual's perceptions and experiences are completely unique, you may uncover dysfunctional patterns in your own past that are specific to yourself; and you will, I hope, find a way to work through them that is right for you as an individual. I encourage you wholeheartedly to find and embrace your own truths, whether or not they are found in the pages of this or any book. Only you can know what is true for yourself, and learning to trust your own instincts is the first step on the path to finding your own truth and creating a life you enjoy.

Once you uncover the origins of your emotional issues and work through them, your interactions with people in the business will become clearer and simpler. You will most likely be more successful in your approach to your profession, and you'll begin to feel more in command in every area of your life. The more awareness you can bring to these issues, and the more you can release the negative emotions surrounding them, the more focus, control, and satisfaction you'll have in your life and throughout your career.

HOW TO USE THIS BOOK

As you read through this book, pay special attention to the specific areas of the business that bother you. Try to discern whether your feelings in these areas are *familiar* feelings, and when you can identify them, search your past for their roots, the causal factors. If a particular experience from your past comes up in your memory, that experience may be where a pattern of behavior began for you. Discovering the link between past and present feelings often causes an "Ah-hah!" response—you'll know when you've found a truth for yourself—so feel free to trust your instincts in this work.

It also helps to learn to identify and put a name to the feelings that come up surrounding these issues. In dysfunctional families, much of the confusion begins before a child learns to communicate verbally, and some of these feelings may have been closed off before you could give a name to them. The clearer you can get about exactly what you are feeling, the easier it is to understand and let go of that feeling. For example, does the lack of response to you in the business make you angry? Or sad? Does it make you feel that you might as well not even bother? Do you feel cheated? What other feelings come up for you? By differentiating and naming the feelings that are specific to you, you can begin to gain an extraordinary understanding of your deepest self, of who you were as a child as well as who you've become.

Half the battle in this kind of work is simply recognizing the connections between your present feelings and your past experiences. Once you can pinpoint the similarities, you can release the old feelings and clear the way for new and better experiences. This kind of work can also be very instrumental in expanding and deepening your talent and technique: As you get more in touch with your inner self, you'll have many more resources to draw on in your acting work.

As you read through the interviews, if something strikes you as a problem you have experienced or are currently struggling with, take a few moments to reflect on that. Validate for yourself that you are not the only one who has that problem, that others are often as uncertain as you are. And take time to explore your responses to the interviews. Often, knowing that others are experiencing the same kinds of feelings will allow you to feel more comfortable with your own feelings.

As you read through the book and work with the Exercises, be open to your own instincts as to the best way, for you as an individual, to approach these emotional explorations. Always treat your feelings with respect and gentleness, just as you would treat a hurt child. Your feelings are there for a reason, whether they arose from early wounds and frustrations or are results of your current experiences. They come from a very deep and vulnerable part of you, so it's best if you can provide yourself with a complete sense of safety and security whenever you are dealing with your feelings. The Exercises are intended to help you discover and release feelings you may not have been in touch with for a long time, so take your time and work on them at your own pace, in whatever way is most comfortable for you. The more you can explore and understand your feelings, the more you will learn about yourself, your perception of the world, and what it is you really want.

The important thing to remember is to follow your own instincts. If you suddenly think you might like to try an Exercise in a slightly different way, or if you think of a new way to work through your response patterns or solve a problem, go with it! These kinds of thoughts and feelings usually come from the most intelligent and natural part of your self, and this natural intelligence at your core will begin to guide you to work in the way that is best for you. If you quickly think, "That's not the way I'm supposed to do it," or "That's a stupid idea," you could be repeating an experience of shaming from childhood that created problems you have today.

The more you can listen to your intuition, the more you will learn about yourself and your view of the world. Your intuitions may be speaking to you very softly at first (and sometimes the ideas you come up with might seem a bit odd to begin with), but if you listen carefully and honor them as much as you can, they will lead you in directions that will help you to express yourself in your own, unique way—as an actor, as a business person, and as a human being.

CHAPTER ONE

THE BIGGEST BARRIER: FEAR

As an actor, you've chosen a career in which it is imperative to face your fears. Acting itself requires a tremendous amount of courage; most people would never set foot on a stage, let alone reveal their innermost feelings in front of a crowd. Stage fright can unfortunately metamorphose from a natural instinct, which is to be wary of revealing oneself, to a fear of the business—the risks and uncertainties inherent in the building of an acting career. Actors must audition day after day, week after week, in a never-ending process of looking for work. The anxiety involved in going to auditions and interviews can range from a slight tension that dulls the work a bit to an overwhelming fear of losing everything if the audition or interview does not go well.

It's important to realize that there are many, many people in the business, and that there will be many, many chances to show yourself and your work. Especially now, companies in every field are changing rapidly, and there's a fairly large turnover in the business. Many agents and casting directors move from job to job; people leave the business; new people enter the business. Opportunities in cable, video, and interactive media are expanding rapidly, and these fields will most likely continue to grow. There will always be more chances, more possibilities, for showing your work, as you grow in your skills and abilities.

WHAT WILL PEOPLE THINK?

A lot of fear stems from worrying about what other people think of you. As a child, you may have seen your parents experience anxiety over other people's opinions, or you may have even actually heard, "What will people think?" This anxiety can particularly affect you as an actor because the image a person cultivates in the business seems very important, and fear of what others think can cause you to freeze up when you're around someone in a powerful position. But even though some casting people hold a certain amount of power, no single casting director, agent, director, or producer is going to make or break your career. Instead of worrying about other people's opinions, concentrate on the kind of work you want to do. The problem with worrying about other people's opinions, in any business, is that they are based on individual perspectives which may be totally different from yours. Even if you do try to conform to what you think someone else wants, you'll run into problems when you get to the next person, who will probably have another, entirely different, opinion. You could find yourself, after a while, trying to do things twenty different ways to please twenty different people and getting confused and frustrated.

The best choice is usually to follow your own instincts, or to spend some time developing them if you're unsure yet of what they are.

It can be tough and frightening to try to find and follow your own truth, especially in a business where others seem to make all the rules. Most of us were brought up to follow guidelines that others set out for us, rather than creating our own way of being and doing. Fear often arises out of concern about "following the rules," but in reality there aren't any rules for building an acting career, no set path that will guarantee success. The best path to follow is your own—one that you create yourself, one that will lead you to a happier and more fulfilling life. This will reflect positively on your talent, as well as the way you're perceived by others in the business.

MOVING BEYOND FEAR

One way to move beyond fear and regain a sense of personal power is to step back a bit and examine what drives you to pursue an acting career. The most important question to ask yourself is "What exactly do I want to get out of this?" It may require some inward searching for a time, getting to know yourself more deeply, in order to answer the question truthfully—most people don't look under the surface to find out what kinds of needs are really driving them. Only when you know what you truly want will you be able to discover and create what will make you happy. It's easy to give pat answers to questions about what you want: "I'm doing this because I want to be an actor." But *why exactly* do you want to be an actor? In other words, what do you hope to get out of it? Do you want attention from other people? Do you want to feel important? Use your intelligence and creativity? Do you especially enjoy exploring characters, living someone else's life for a change, expressing yourself in ways that are new to you? All the reasons you've chosen to be an actor, all the needs that you're trying to meet for yourself, can be met in other areas of life, usually less fearfully and more easily than in the acting business. Determine what you're really looking for and try to find ways to meet your needs in other areas of your life. Your fear will lessen when you're not as dependent on the business and your acting career to bring you satisfaction.

Another way to regain a sense of power is to ask yourself, "Would I like to work with these people?" instead of wondering what those people think of you. This may take a bit of concentration, because we're so oriented towards doing an audition that will land us the job, and trying to give the people sitting out there in the dark what we think they're looking for. We forget to consider whether or not we'd like to work with them (sometimes we find out that we don't really want to!). This change in perspective is extremely important to your self-esteem as an actor and as a business person. "What do *I* think of *them*?" will help hone your sense of the types of people you'd enjoy working with and the kinds of projects you'd like to do. It will help you see that you're not powerless, that you don't need to be afraid, and that you do have options. When you're thinking "Will they like me?" you may end up feeling you're not worthwhile—as an actor or as a person—unless you get the job.

Perfection Is Not a Realistic Goal

Another response pattern related to the audition or interview is the feeling that you need to achieve perfection. This again is a fear that can stem from a sense of powerlessness often related to childhood experiences. Do you customarily berate yourself after auditions for anything that didn't happen exactly as you wanted? If so, you may have a problem with this pattern. The need to achieve perfection is closely connected to the feeling that you must "follow the rules" in order to get what you want:

• When you were a child, were there certain set ways of doing things that you had to follow?

• Did others often push you to do better, to do more?

• Were you made to feel bad if you made a mistake or didn't do the job "well enough"?

Mistakes are natural in any effort to achieve—sometimes the only way to discover the best method is to find out first what doesn't work. There are few situations in life in which you can say, "This is completely and perfectly done." And it can be frustrating to try to achieve something when there are no rules to follow, no end point at which everything is ideal and complete. This is not to suggest that you shouldn't do the best you can at things that are important to you, but there often is a point, if you stop and look at the situation, where your efforts have been "good enough." Take some time to discover where you feel you need to be perfect, and try stepping back to see if things are good enough as they are. There will always be things that are frustrating in life, and there will always be some times when you don't get what you want—life always includes both sides of the coin, good and bad. There is no way to control how things will turn out, and there is no way to make everything perfect. Learn to be comfortable with the idea that things don't have to be perfect in order for you to feel good about yourself and your life.

As a child, you may have been afraid the world would come tumbling down if you weren't perfect or didn't achieve exactly the result that you or someone else wanted. But as an adult, you have enough experience to know that life goes on, no matter what happens, and that there are other, more enjoyable pursuits than striving for perfection. If you find yourself trying to achieve perfection in any area of your life, it can be very helpful to do some thinking about your past to find out why. If you don't examine the fears and experiences of your "inner child," you'll probably continue to respond to your current experiences from that childhood perspective, rather than as an adult in command of your life.

It's always good to examine yourself and your work in order to improve and grow, but if the examination is based on "what you did wrong," you'll only hold yourself back from achieving the best that you can achieve.

There is no scale with which to measure perfection in a performance, audition, or interview. In fact, there are usually a number of different ways to create a desired effect, not just a single "perfect" one. If you're constantly striving to "do it right," you will only hamper your creativity and growth.

The following suggestions can help you increase your self-esteem and regain some of your own power:

- Talk to yourself in supportive ways rather than putting yourself down.

- Give yourself credit for the things you do well.

- If you feel you've made a mistake, forgive yourself and move on, and expect that you'll do better the next time.

- Instead of reaching for some undefinable standard of perfection, strive to be yourself, please yourself, and do the best work that you can.

Resolving Your Fears

One of the best ways to move beyond fear is to stop trying to figure out what people are looking for. Not only is it an impossible task, but most of the time, *they* don't even know what they're looking for. Casting people will have only a general idea of the possibilities for a particular role and will be looking for something that they can't really put their finger on until they see it. If you think you've figured out what they're looking for and change yourself to conform to that, you may be cutting off the very uniqueness in yourself that might get you a callback—the very quirk that could land you the job.

If you can be yourself and find ways to enjoy auditions and interviews, you'll gain much more freedom in your acting and discover new ways to respond to the people you're auditioning for. Do the work in order to satisfy the artist within you, rather than to appease others. Please yourself in the monologues you choose and in the way you perform them. It's impossible to second-guess others, and even if you could, you might end up somewhere you don't want to be. Follow your own instincts and do work you enjoy doing—otherwise, you'll find yourself dissatisfied in the long run, tired of the acting you used to love.

If you try to shape yourself and your talent to what you think others want, you are seeking their approval, and if you don't get it, this can lead to a lack of self-esteem. Learn to approve of yourself in every possible way. You have every right to be in this life pursuing an acting career, and self-esteem can only come from within—from learning to please yourself and to love yourself the way you are, no matter what happens in the business or in your career. Besides, a lot of other actors are trying to please casting people. If you try to please them too, you'll look like too many of the others. If you learn to please yourself, you'll stand out as a unique, confident, bold individual. And if your objective is to please yourself rather than someone else, you'll probably find that auditions and interviews don't generate so much fear for you, because they're no longer about what the other person thinks. The more you search for ways to make the process enjoyable for yourself, the less you'll be frightened of not making a good impression.

When you're working on audition pieces by yourself, or when you're on the way home from an audition, you may be able to resolve some of your fears just by looking at them more closely. Although it can be a bit unnerving to explore these issues—it may seem like there's an endless well of emotion to contend with—in the long run you can achieve much more freedom and enjoyment by dealing with your emotional issues now, rather than continually pushing them to the back of your mind. If you avoid paying attention to these kinds of issues, they will end up controlling you in an unconcious way, causing you to do and say things automatically, rather than by a concious choice.

Try to discover for yourself exactly what you're most afraid of in an audition. Be gentle with yourself as you explore—you may be connecting with a deeper and more vulnerable part of yourself. Are you afraid of . . .

• Making a fool of yourself or being ridiculed?

• Not being able to get or keep the person's attention?

• Exposing a vulnerable part of yourself?

• Not being liked?

Sometimes our fears are out of proportion to the reality of the situation. This seems to be somewhat normal in our society, so if it's true for you, you're not alone. But often, intense fears come from some past experience or a feeling that has never been resolved and keeps popping up to get your attention. If you're afraid of a specific event, such as incurring someone's wrath, or of being judged in a negative way, ask yourself if there is an experience, or a set of experiences, in your past that could have caused you to be afraid.

• Did someone in your family get angry when you tried to state your mind or do what you wanted to do?

• Did someone always "pass judgment" on your behavior or accomplishments?

• Did you have a teacher who humiliated you if you gave the wrong answer?

• Were you ridiculed by a family member if you didn't do what he or she wanted?

Take some time to search your memory for feelings or experiences that are similar to the current problem you're working on, letting your instincts guide you. Eventually you'll notice that certain feelings are familiar to you on a very deep level. These are the areas you need to investigate; they will bring the most richness and depth to your life—and to your acting.

As you begin to focus on these early situations, try to release any feelings that come up for you. (See the "Exercises to Build Self-Esteem," beginning on page 162, for help in releasing the feelings.) When you discover feelings from the past that are negatively affecting you in a present situation, it's helpful to remind yourself that the original experience is part of the past, and that you have many more options now as an adult.

Everyone's past is different, but we all carry memories of experiences from our childhood that affect our perceptions and the way we interact with others. The more discoveries you can make as to why you fear certain situations, and the more you can release feelings that are getting in your way, the less your fear will rule your life.

FEAR AS A FACADE

Fear can also be a cover-up for other emotions, a sort of buffer to keep you from experiencing things on a deeper level. It can be a cover for anger or rage, especially if you were afraid, or were not allowed to express these feelings when you were young. Fear is the organism's natural response to something that seems threatening, whether it comes from inner feelings that are too threatening to look at or from outside the self. The key is to explore your feelings a little at a time, until you get more comfortable with them and with helping yourself understand them. As you begin to uncover some of your earliest feelings, keep an eye out for feelings of anger and rage that may be mixed in with fear, or feelings of fear that are hidden underneath your anger.

At some point in your childhood, your feelings of fear and excitement might have become confused. Excitement itself can be overwhelming to a young child, and the feeling of being overwhelmed can generate fear. Moreover, adults may have felt threatened when you got excited about something and may have gotten angry or acted in a threatening way toward you, causing you fear. In the atmosphere of your childhood, perhaps fear was allowed or even encouraged ("Be careful on the way home!"), but excitement was not ("Calm down! There's nothing to get excited about!"). The next time you feel scared about something, ask yourself if you might actually be excited as well. Don't try to *change* the fear into excitement; just look under the surface, check out the feeling, and see if the fear is a cover-up or replacement for a different emotion.

Fear can also hold you back from exploration and growth. Family messages about the dangers of exploring new possibilities and growing beyond the "family circle" can be very strong. It can appear to threaten the family system if one member is behaving in new and unexpected ways. As you begin to examine your fears and their causes, ask yourself whether or not you were encouraged to explore. What kind of messages did you get about exploring or growing? How did you feel when you did explore something new or go beyond what was expected? If you fear trying something new, let yourself explore it a little at a time, allowing yourself the freedom to back off until you feel safe again, then exploring a bit further. Small steps in this area can help you learn to feel safe while you explore, so that you can move beyond your fear. Trying to take large steps will usually exacerbate the fear and may make the situation worse for you.

WHO INTIMIDATES YOU?

Certain people seem to make us freeze up, even when there is no identifiable reason for our fear. If certain people in the business seem to intimidate you more than others, look again at your past: Does that particular person remind you of anyone? The resemblance doesn't have to be physical—it can be a tone of voice or a way of treating you. Try to discover what it is that makes you freeze up, and see if the feeling is familiar from long ago. (It's best to do this work when your mind is free to concentrate on yourself. It's not the kind of work to do at an actual audition, where you must be in the present moment and concentrate on doing the best job of acting that you can.)

One thing that's very important to know is that it is not okay for anyone to abuse you (even if it's just verbal abuse)—not teachers, or coaches, or anyone who might hire you. A teacher's job is to support you and help you learn and grow, not to undermine your confidence. Some people in positions of power in this business hold their jobs basically because they enjoy having power over others. Actors are some of the best people there are, in terms of sensitivity, intelligence, willingness to please, and friendliness, and they can easily fall prey to manipulators simply because they want so much to make the contact or get the job. Remember that you don't have to do whatever they say, and you don't have to let people use you as an outlet for their anger and frustration, no matter what they tell you, and no matter what they seem to have to offer.

If you have experienced this problem, you may be hiding your own anger and frustration behind a fear of more abuse. Many people were mistakenly taught as they grew up that others had a right to invalidate or yell at them, and you may feel a certain "familiarity" with this kind of situation if that was true for you. However, allowing others to treat you badly as an adult not only damages self-esteem and exacerbates fear; it can also harm your acting talent and skills. The more you stand up for yourself—leaving, for example, if a situation is too abusive—the more your self-esteem and confidence will grow. There are always other people and other teachers to work with; there are always future possibilities. Not everyone in the business is out to mistreat actors, and if you choose not to let the abusers mistreat you, you'll begin to find people just like yourself who are really in it for the art and the human connection. If you tolerate abuse and allow it to continue, over time you'll come to resent the business and eventually lose your passion for your art.

The more you can explore your fears and discover the roots of your own anxiety, the freer you'll become in terms of both the business and your acting technique. We all want to be confident and courageous all the time, but it's just not possible: Life is too complex a mix of all kinds of sensations and experiences. What does change as you begin to explore the undercurrents of your feelings about the business is your attitude toward yourself:

- You'll feel more powerful and decisive because you'll have a better idea of exactly what you want and how to go about getting it.

- You'll see yourself more as an equal to those "in power," and less as one who should obey, fear, or worship them.

- You'll feel less frightened and powerless, more sure of yourself and your choices.

Don't be afraid to follow your heart—a lot of what society deems "abnormal" or "wrong" comes from collective fears of individuality and the instinctual self. If it feels right to you, it probably is worth a try.

As you begin to compare your feelings and experiences in the present with those in your past, you'll find similarities which can help you to unlock the hold the past has on your unconcious mind. The more you can understand the negative patterns from the past and their influence on your current experiences, the easier it will become to recognize them, work through them, and regain control over your life and career.

CHAPTER TWO

REJECTION: THE BIG STING

In the business of acting, the experience of rejection is often the only constant. People in most other fields come up against it only a few times in their careers as they interview for jobs, but actors must deal with rejection day after day throughout their careers. Understanding the emotional issues surrounding rejection can make it much easier to deal with.

Everyone knows what it's like to feel rejected. Many of these feelings may originate in childhood, particularly during the "terrible twos"—when we want so many things that just aren't possible and are often told "no" when we reach for something we desire. As children learn more and more about the world and the possibilities it holds, they reach for more and more of the new things around them. Up to the age of two, physical needs have generally been met without fail by a parent or parents: Children are fed and bathed and usually attended to when they cry. But when they begin to move out into the world, expecting the same constant fulfillment of their needs, parents are no longer able to meet every demand. In order to get through the "terrible twos" stage, many parents will unequivocally keep saying "no" to almost every demand their toddlers make, simply to ensure that they will finally understand that the parents are in charge and that they can't have everything they want.

As a result of this "indoctrination," children can end up feeling unacceptable, simply because most or all of their desires, which come from the center of their being, are denied. Then, as they grow and become adults, every time they experience rejection these early feelings of unworthiness arise again. A pattern of response surrounding feelings of rejection develops.

To the actor, each and every audition can seem like a possible chance to get the attention and respect he or she may not have gotten as a child, yet feels is deserved. If you're not getting the respect and attention you need from your family, friends, or even yourself, you'll necessarily continue to seek that from every audition; and every time you don't get called back, you'll experience major disappointment, because once again your "inner child" has been thwarted in terms of getting your needs met.

There's a real danger in putting the core of your inner self on the line for your acting career in this way. The business is extremely competitive, and unless you're lucky enough to start and stay working within a short period of time, chances are that your self-esteem will plummet if you base your sense of self-worth on whether or not you're getting a good response to your auditions and marketing efforts.

This isn't to say that you shouldn't approach your career with passion and determination—it usually takes a tremendous amount of both of these qualities to get a career rolling. But when you base your sense of self-worth entirely on whether or not your career is going well, your feelings of self-worth are liable to go up and down like a roller-coaster, following the peaks and valleys that are a natural part of every actor's career. In order to have a healthy sense of self-esteem, you need to shift your focus onto yourself as a person, not just as an actor. You are much more than the skills (the "product") you are marketing, much more than simply an actor—just as there is much more in you than you would bring to a particular role. The qualities in yourself that you'd make use of in creating a Cleopatra or Macbeth are still parts of you when you're living your life or performing a very different kind of role—in *Oklahoma,* for instance, or *Broadway Bound*—whether or not you're aware of them on a day-to-day basis. They are all facets of your inner self, and each is as important as the other. These qualities are not just a reflection of your acting talent; they are part of who you are as a person.

Take time to appreciate yourself as a person. Learn to cultivate the many wondrous aspects of yourself, and honor each of them. They are the human heart of you. You may use them in your acting, but don't base your esteem and appreciation of the myriad parts of yourself on whether you get a particular role or make it in the acting business. You are important and wonderful just for who you are, not for whether or not you're a successful actor. The more you honor yourself as a person, the more likely it is that you'll be successful in whatever field you choose.

SELF AND PRODUCT: NOT THE SAME THING

One problem specific to actors is that the rejection experienced in the business can become personalized. In other words, if you are rejected as an actor for a certain role, you may feel as if you yourself are being rejected. The problem, of course, is that an actor uses him- or herself in acting, so it's easy to feel rejected when you and the "product" both live in the same body. If you are confusing the image you're presenting in the business with your true self and your career is not moving forward as quickly as you expect or desire, it can affect your life to the degree that you feel less and less confident in other areas of your life, less and less able to take care of yourself in a larger sense. Understanding that you are not being rejected as a person when you don't get a callback or role is a very important distinction to make for yourself.

Acting is different from arts like painting and writing, because an actor creates a work of art that is inseparable from the self. A painter can paint a picture and produce art in total seclusion and then hold his or her creation up for others to see: "This is what I created." A writer can write a story or play, and when it becomes a written and/or published physical entity apart from him- or herself, others read it. There is "space" between the creator and the created entity.

If the painter's or writer's work is rejected, even though it comes from his or her own heart, mind, and artistic sense, it is still a thing outside of the self—there is distance between the artist and the art. But when an actor is creating, the actor is the "painting"—there is no material work of art outside the self which represents the act of creation. For actors, then, it can feel as if the self is being rejected when they are not chosen for the role. The physical body, the mind, and the emotions are felt to be rejected.

The problem is compounded by the fact that actors are constantly working to deepen and sensitize the "instrument," so that it responds appropriately at the right time. If you find yourself feeling very sensitive or vulnerable every time you don't get called back or cast, it may be that you are taking the rejection personally, rather than realizing it's more a matter of which actor the casting person believes would be best for the role—always a subjective decision. You have trained your instrument—your body, mind, and emotions—for the craft of acting, not for dealing with the ups and downs of the business. It's important to keep these aspects of your career separate.

This is confusing, naturally, because of the nature of the acting business: You go into an audition, meet the casting person, and then use your self through your craft when you're acting. It can be difficult to turn your technique on and off, but the casting person doesn't want to meet your sense memory and emotional needs when you come in the door. He or she more likely hopes you'll save that for your acting and just be an interesting person who's enjoyable to meet. Keep your needs quiet when you introduce yourself, then let them fly when you're acting. This isn't to say that you must be two different people, schizophrenic, or phony, just that you can first be more connected with the warm, intelligent, or vivacious (however you are as an individual) side of your personality as you meet the person, and then be more in touch with that core of yourself from which your acting talent flows while you're doing a monologue or reading a scene. And when you walk out the door, let your body and mind quiet again as much as you can, and go on with your life.

You may feel a letdown after an audition or interview, even one that you felt went well. In part this is because acting involves being in a heightened state of feeling and awareness, so that when you move back into your real life after the audition, you may feel depressed. It may also have to do with the fact that you're doing what you love most—acting—for two minutes or less, building yourself up to a peak so that you do your best, and having such a short period of time to present your work. The best way to keep yourself from getting depressed after an audition is to schedule something you enjoy immediately following the audition: getting together with a friend, shopping, or having a good meal—whatever usually cheers you up. This can also help you see that living your life is more important than how your career is going. There are, after all, good times to be had in other ways besides acting.

EARLY REJECTION OF FEELINGS

There is a strong tendency in our society, and in most families, to hide and ignore feelings, and the rejection that is an integral part of the acting business can seem to be a replaying of the past, when others either rejected your feelings or shamed you for having them.

The intense feelings that children often have can be very threatening to adults, especially if the adults also had their own feelings mishandled when they were small. Feelings are so much a part of human nature that if they are cut off or unexpressed, a large and potentially glorious part of our being is hidden away, unused and undiscovered. The more you can get in touch with your feelings, the richer your life and your acting will become.

Emotional issues that come up for you surrounding rejection as an actor may be a reflection of your childhood history and/or your family's attitude toward feelings:

- When you were a child, did you get messages that it was wrong or bad to have feelings?

- How did the adults in your family respond to your feelings?

- Did you see the adults around you express feelings?

- Did adults express a full range of feelings, or in only one or two areas?

As an actor, you've chosen a field in which others expect and encourage you to work with your feelings. You may have decided to be an actor partly because it offers an opportunity to explore and express feelings that you might not feel safe with in real life, where most people tend to hide or ignore their feelings.

If you're auditioning a lot, but getting little work, it may feel as if your emotions are once again being rejected by others.

The best way to overcome this problem is to bring your feelings into your conscious mind so that you can look at them and "own" them, accept them fully as being your feelings. That way, you can accept them yourself even if others seem to be rejecting or ignoring them.

Also, take a look at your family's current response to your decision to be an actor. If you come from a non-arts background, if members of your family have usually worked regularly at 9-to-5 jobs, it may be difficult for them to accept the unconventional and unpredictable life-style actors usually have. If this is true, you may experience rejection from them as well concerning your choice of acting as a career. It can be difficult to convince them that you truly are building a career when you only work occasionally as an actor and spend much of the rest of your time either pursuing acting work or working at a job such as waiting tables or word processing. If you're able to talk openly with your family, it can be helpful to take some time to explain your situation to them and to express your feelings. But if you feel that there's no way you could make them understand, consider the following:

- You have the right to do what you want with your life.

- You can neither change others, nor do you exist to fulfill other people's expectations. Your own happiness is what's most important.

- You can create and nurture supportive relationships with others in the business so that you're not dependent on your family for approval and validation.

BEING OBJECTIVE ABOUT REJECTION

There are ways you can handle rejection in the business much less stress-fully: Most helpful is simply to take a more objective view, to realize that the rejection is not based on who you are or how much talent you have. It has nothing to do with you personally, but is simply a fact of life for an actor pursuing a career. Roles are not necessarily cast on the basis of talent—there may be many other factors involved. Almost always, large numbers of other actors are also audiitioning, and this lowers your chance of being cast.

Take a moment immediately after each audition or interview to remind yourself that you are a valuable and worthy person, whether or not you get a callback or job. This may sound trite, and you may at first experience a resistance to trying something so simple, but after a few reminders that your importance and value are not based on getting the role, the pressure surrounding auditions and interviews will begin to lessen. You'll start to connect with a deeper part of yourself. As you begin to give yourself the attention and respect you deserve, your perspective on the business will clear and widen, and you'll begin to find ways to experience more satisfaction and success.

Another way to better handle rejection is to delve into your past and uncover old feelings you may be hiding from yourself:

• Does it bother you to think that people are judging you every time you audition?

• Is the feeling you get when you've auditioned for a role, but not been called back, a familiar one?

• Can you put your finger on what it reminds you of?

• Do you feel it's nearly impossible to get what you want, even before you start trying?

• Do you feel like you have to work really hard to get or maintain someone's attention?

These questions all point to feelings you may have carried into your experience of the business from early childhood. Spend some time thinking about your responses to being judged or rejected and try to release any feelings that may be getting in your way (see the Exercises). Begin to notice the times you do get what you want—for instance, when someone answers your questions. We often tend to focus on the times we don't get what we want, rather than the times we do. And begin to find ways to give yourself small things that you want—a bouquet of flowers, a day at the seashore—and focus on the fact that as an adult, you don't need to depend so much on others. You're now more able to give yourself more of what you want.

Business Is Just Business

It's also helpful to get a broader perspective of what business is really about. Imagine, for instance, that you run a business selling lampshades. A prospective customer may decide to buy someone else's lampshade instead of yours. You probably wouldn't have much of a sense of rejection, at least not on a personal level. You might try to find out why customers choose other lampshades over yours, or you might decide to change your own product to make it more desirable. Every actor's essence is unique—there are many varieties, just as there are many different lampshades. Thus, casting people have a wide range of options. If you don't get a role, it's probably not because of any shortcoming on your part; it's simply that the casting person chose an actor with a different "essence," just as a decorator may choose one lampshade over another.

The key is to remember that the rejection is not a reflection on you as a person and is probably not even a reflection on you as an actor; it's just a matter of the wide variety of available actors. First, try to recognize that your feelings surrounding rejection are probably fed by the past; second, understand that your feelings are then exacerbated by the realities of numbers in the business; and, third, learn to value yourself more as a person. Your confidence will grow, and you'll feel happier with your life.

Rejection is one of the most important patterns to work through, because it will happen time after time after time in your career, even if you are incredibly talented and lucky. And if the problem isn't dealt with early on, it can eventually develop into extreme bitterness and cynicism, or you may come to fear rejection so much over time that you hide more and more of your inner self, leaving less and less of your uniqueness available for your acting and your life. The rejection pattern, like any other, changes little by little, step by step; over time, as you learn to be good to yourself in every way you can, you'll be happier and more connected with yourself and the world around you. Rejection in the business will then bother you less and less.

Allow yourself to feel and express the disappointment of rejection, treat yourself well, and work to develop your self-esteem—this combination will help you take the sting out of the rejection you'll face throughout your career.

CHAPTER THREE

DEALING WITH PEOPLE IN POWER

Agents, casting directors, producers, and directors can appear to be extremely powerful people who are more important to the success of your career than anything else. Many of them have worked hard to achieve their positions and struggled to be the best they can be in the field, but they are often thought by actors to have more power than they actually do. None of them, no matter what their position, can make an actor a star or even know for certain whether or not a particular actor will be successful—there are too many variables. And even the most well-connected agent can only arrange auditions for you. It's still up to you to get the job.

In the last ten years, the business has changed dramatically, partly because of the large numbers of actors coming into the business and partly because of general economic trends. Because there is usually a time shortage in the casting process, casting directors generally bring in actors whose work they are familiar with, rather than searching for new faces. Agents rarely take on a new client unless that actor is already well on the way to success. More common is the freelance relationship, a trial period in which the agent sends a new actor on a few auditions. But if the actor doesn't book a job quickly, the trial period can be over in a few months. Some agents will even freelance with a new face "just in case" that actor becomes successful.

Sadly, but truly, a lot of work in the acting business, especially at higher levels, is based on whom you know more than on the talent you have. Stories abound of actors who have made it because someone in their family is in the business. This would seem to indicate to the actor who has no such connections that he or she should quickly meet as many people as possible. The danger here is that you may feel it's so urgent to meet people that you overlook the real point, which is to connect with others on a personal level. There are always going to be some people you hit it off with and some you don't, just as it is in life. When you do meet someone new, take the time to notice your own feelings:

• Does this person treat you and others with respect?

• Is this a person whose values and work you respect?

• If not, do you feel you can still do business with them in an ethical way?

Your own ethics may also be something you need to examine: Do you treat others with respect? No one likes to be approached as just another name to add to your networking list. Try to develop an interest in other people, a curiosity about what makes them tick. Ask about and listen to their experiences and ideas—don't just rattle off a list of your credits to try to impress them. The business is built on personal connections, so be open to others as much as you can. If someone doesn't connect with you, respect that fact, and look for others who are more on your wavelength.

AGENTS AND CASTING DIRECTORS AS AUTHORITY FIGURES

One of the reasons that agents and casting people can seem so powerful is that your perception of them may be similar to the way you perceived your parents and teachers when you were small: They knew a lot more than you did, simply because they'd been in the world a lot longer. You may have even felt that they knew secrets about things, because they seemed to have all the answers, while you were unsure. They were also physically bigger than you were, which meant you literally looked up to them. Adults and older siblings—the authority figures in your life—had a tremendous amount of power: the power to help you get what you wanted, or to withhold it, or even to try to make you do certain things or behave in certain ways before they would give you what you wanted. The feeling you have today that casting people and agents are all-powerful is a good example of the way that childhood experiences can influence your present-day acting pursuits.

Your childhood perceptions were natural—for a child. If adults don't take the time to guide children into learning how to find the answers, but just tell them what to do, they may grow up believing that others always know more than they do. This can lead to the feeling that without the help and guidance of an authority figure (for instance, an agent or casting person), there is no chance to succeed, or that there is some secret to success, when there really is not. These childhood perceptions will only hold you back, as an adult, from connecting with others and making your own choices.

Actors often believe that casting directors, agents, directors, and producers have power to such an extent that they can make us happy or make our lives and struggles worthwhile. They can seem to be substitute parent figures: people who can take care of us and give us what we want, people who will show us the way to succeed. But they do not have all the power; in fact, they're just as worried about getting the next job for themselves or their clients as actors are—and, of course, they wouldn't have jobs at all if there were no actors. Granted, some people are manipulators, on a "power trip," out to take advantage of actors. If you learn to trust your gut instincts, you can usually avoid them.

The only way to stop feeling powerless about your own ability to make a difference in your career is to relinquish the illusion that "they" have all the power, that only "they" can give you the career you want. If you continue to maintain the illusion that "they" have all the power, your fear of rejection can increase, and auditions and interviews can become more frightening and frustrating. Again, this illusion is a reflection of your most basic childhood experience. The problem can usually be resolved by thinking back and asking some questions about your past:

- When you were a child, did you feel that authority figures helped you get what you wanted?

- Or, instead, did they withhold objects or attention from you?

- Did you feel that they had all the power and you had none at all?

- Did you feel they tried to manipulate you in order to get you to do what they wanted?

Exploring your feelings in this area can help you discover some of the early experiences which influenced your present perceptions about authority figures, and to move beyond believing that someone else must determine whether or not you get what you want.

A particularly sticky pattern of response that can arise from the past is the belief (express or implied) that you might possibly get what you want if you do a particular thing or things—as if you had been promised positive results. Marketing yourself as an actor and developing connections with agents and casting people can seem to duplicate this particular pattern. Of course, there are no guarantees in life, but in your family this kind of "strings-attached" promise may have been used to get you to behave in a certain way. Then the reward may not have been given, leaving you with the feeling that you have to do every single thing that someone else wants, just so that there will be even a slight possibility of getting what you want. This pattern, which is similar to many actors' present-day experiences, creates an enormous feeling of powerlessness. Even if you do the required things, you may still not get what you want—and, usually, there is no other way to get what you want, so you have no control.

Check your past: Did you feel you had requirements to fulfill, established by others, in order to get anything for yourself? If you were brought up with this pattern, you may be giving up your power without thinking, without even trying to get what you want in *alternative* ways. Remember that, as an adult, you always have a choice in the matter and you don't any longer have to do as anyone else says. Remind yourself that you have life experience and intelligence just like anyone else, and find ways to create new paths to what you want, rather than following someone else's suggestions or demands.

It can be very helpful to examine your general perceptions about agents, casting directors, producers, and directors:

- Do you feel as if they have the ability to give you what you want, if you could only figure out how to please them?

- Do you feel that you have to behave a certain way around them?

- Must you perhaps even *hide* your decisiveness, vulnerability, strength (or other traits) when you're around them?

If this strikes a chord for you, you may be perceiving agents, casting directors, producers, and directors as parental figures, responding to them in much the same way that you responded to your parents when you were small. It's important to understand that they are just people like everyone else—grocers, librarians, construction workers—and that they were children once, too. The same is true of other professionals you're working with who have made a name for themselves. It will help you tremendously if you can take them down off of the pedestal in your mind, and see them more as fellow human beings you might enjoy knowing than as people who hold power over you.

There are some people in positions of power in the business who may have chosen the work they do precisely because they need to feel they have power over others. When this is the case, their behavior often has its origins in childhood as well. Unfortunately, actors can be a prime target for this kind of person, simply because there are so many actors seeking so few jobs, and this creates an imbalance. If you feel that someone is not respecting you as a person, or if you have even the slightest inkling that you're being abused in some way, it's very important to look at your feelings regarding the situation:

• Does it feel familiar to you?

• Did someone in your past treat you this way?

• How did you feel about it then?

• How do you feel about it now?

Regardless of whether this kind of situation is similar to one in your past or reflects what you believe the business to be like, it serves no positive purpose whatsoever for you to put up with any kind of disrespect. The longer you do, the faster your self-esteem will erode.

If you did have an experience like this as a child, it could possibly feel comfortable, perhaps even safe, to you. To help you see the situation without distortion, you might consider finding a therapist or support group. You might want to talk with others who are in the same position you are in. Do they feel that they get the same kinds of responses from a given person?

You do not have to consent to mistreatment. Instead, you should feel free to take your business to someone you respect and who treats you with regard. Help and guidance can be the best thing in the world if it comes from a good source. But letting someone force you to do anything or talk you into a position that goes against your better instincts will never be worth it in the long run.

You know more than you think you do. It's just a matter of realizing that you are now an adult with many more options than you had as a child. You have an incredible amount of life experience to help and guide you. This doesn't mean you have all the answers, but learning to trust your instincts and feelings can help you to find your way in life without being dependent on others. Learn to develop your curiosity and natural intelligence, and don't be afraid to test, retest, and experiment with the ideas you come up with. Everyone learns naturally by trial and error, if given the chance.

BECOME YOUR OWN AUTHORITY FIGURE

A lot of us gave up on experimenting and testing a long time ago. The adults we were with may have shamed us for making a mistake or for doing something different from what they wanted or expected. In fact, a lot of what others may have told you were mistakes may simply have been your own way of doing things, a way that didn't fit in with someone else's view of how they should be done. Religion, in particular, often promotes a rigid set of rules that one must follow in order to be "in the right" (in effect, to be loved) or to pass inspection on Judgment Day (that is, to be safe). If you were brought up in a strongly religious atmosphere, you may be particularly afraid to try things your own way and experiment with life.

Most people were taught or shown erroneous rules and beliefs by authority figures simply because the authority figures themselves had been wrongly taught, through many generations. What is important is not finding someone to blame, but moving beyond the past and discovering your own values and beliefs. Learning to live your life by your own rules is, in essence, becoming your own parent, your own authority figure.

It can be very helpful to examine the beliefs you were brought up with in *every* area, to find out if you're still following rules that might not be useful for you any longer. Most children are so inundated with rules and regulations that any natural form of self-expression or discovery can be completely shut off, and you may be following some of these childhood rules in your approach to the business, where they may not be applicable. Try to uncover some of the spoken and unspoken rules in your family, and examine your feelings toward them:

• Do you still feel that a particular direction is valid?

• If not, can you figure out a better way, based on your own life experience?

• Or would the rule work better for you with a certain change?

The more you can discover the differences, even if they are subtle, between the rules you were taught as a child and the things you believe in now, the more you will develop a set of values and principles by which to live your life. There is nothing more important than freedom of choice in life, and the more you can examine the rules you were taught, rid yourself of those you no longer believe in, and adopt the values that you choose to live by, the more your life will be your own.

If you can stop responding to people in the business as if they have all the power, and instead try to connect with them in an honest, straightforward, and personal manner, you'll be taking a big step toward moving beyond the past and developing your own power as an individual, and as an actor.

WORKING WITH DIRECTORS

An actor can also run into problems because his or her acting is "manipulated" by others—namely, the director and the other actors, with the guidelines and structure being provided by the writer. When painters work, unless they are in a class, no one tells them how much blue to use or where—they create their paintings entirely on their own. The actor, however, is expected to understand and incorporate any number of directions and suggestions as to how to create the finished product. This in itself can seem to be a direct reflection of patterns from childhood: As children grow, they have a definite need to learn how to do things in their own way, and this may not be allowed or validated by the adults in the family. Around the age of two, children begin to exhibit definite preferences and inclinations, and the adults in the family begin to set boundaries for the child, some of which may be based on distorted beliefs from their own childhood. This can result in feelings of frustration for the child at not being able to do things in an individual way; the child may even be forced to act in ways that are foreign to his or her nature.

If you find yourself having difficulty accepting a director's ideas, one of the reasons may be that you're reminded of early experiences of this kind. The act of creation is an individual process, based on a person's unique experience and perceptions. But when this process of creation is entered into and "manipulated" by other individuals, as it is in film, television, and theater, it may cause you to feel that your talent, or even your deepest self, is not good enough in itself—that you must constantly look to others for approval and direction, even in other areas of your life outside the business. Again, trust your own instincts; you're an adult, and it's up to you to make the choices in your life. Though you may seek some guidance and direction from others, your life is for you to live, and you are the one who should be in command of it.

Working with others toward a common goal can be one of the most enjoyable and fulfilling experiences in life when there is a give-and-take feeling and an atmosphere of mutual support and encouragement. Yet you need to be able to come from a sense of strength within yourself, a sense that you are contributing to the whole, rather than waiting for someone else to tell you what to do.

When working with a director, actors can also be easily reminded of childhood, in that once again someone else has the final say and the natural creative impulses are once again under the scrutiny of an authority figure (depending on the situation). Working with a director may seem subconciously to present a new opportunity for the "inner child" to be listened to, supported, and encouraged. But it is not the director's job to be a therapist or substitute parent for the actor—the director is there to inform the piece with a unified vision and to ensure that everyone works toward a common goal in terms of the production. If you expect the director to satisfy personal needs that are connected with your childhood, the result can be incredible frustration, or even withdrawal, on either or both sides.

If you find yourself in a situation where working with a certain director is frustrating you, first ask yourself if he or she reminds you of any family member, a parent or sibling. Then try to discover whether your current feelings are familiar in terms of your childhood experience. If so, explore the feelings in terms of the situation which originated them when you were small and try to resolve them on your own time, rather than bringing them to rehearsals. Remember that the objective of everyone in putting on a play is to create together the best possible interpretation of the script, not to use the experience to try to heal old wounds.

Of course, some directors will have their own unconscious patterns of response to work through, just as some casting directors and agents do. Again, if someone is mistreating or abusing you, it won't help you in any way to allow it to continue. Because it's usually impossible to change someone else, often the best thing to do if you realize that you're being treated disrespectfully is to end the relationship, or to choose not to work with that person the next time. The only feasible goal is to work on your own patterns, to try to satisfy your own needs in other ways, and to support yourself as much as you can without infringing on the rehearsal process in order to get your own needs met.

A good director will shape and mold the actor's creation of character to best suit the play, and it's usually important to have an objective eye commenting on the creation. But bear in mind always that it is a collaborative effort—you should feel you're creating something that adds to and defines the piece, not as if you're a puppet who is forced to move from one place to another, from one emotion to the next. Often it is precisely the actor's uniqueness and individual talent that can be overrun by a director who feels that a scene has to go a particular way.

If you're experiencing this problem and feeling frustrated, ask yourself if there is anything in your past that reminds you of the situation: Did your family demand that you always do things their way, or did they allow you some freedom to create new ways of accomplishing what you wanted? Did you feel that they really listened to you, heard what you said, and then responded to it in a way that helped you grow, or did they ignore or belittle your creative drives? If you do find something in your past that's reflected in the present, it won't necessarily change the way the director is responding to you. But if you can understand how your past experience is influencing you now, you'll have more options in terms of your own responses to that person. This can help you feel more in command of the situation.

By all means, if you are feeling stifled or pushed and pulled around by a director, ask him or her to talk with you about it—open, honest communication is a good way to move toward the heart and humanity of a piece. And a director won't know how you feel unless you communicate it; you may not even know how you feel until you put it into words. The best way to improve a relationship with another person is to keep the lines of communication open as much as you can.

It's also important to take a look at your own response to criticism in the rehearsal process. Accepting the director's help in creating your role is a natural part of the process, and if you have trouble accepting that help or feel that any suggestion is an implication that you're not good enough, you may be relating to the situation from a past perspective. Looking back on your family, was there someone who often criticized you or made you feel as if nothing you did was good enough? Or was there someone who tried to help you so much that now your first reaction to help is to withdraw? If you had a difficult experience or situation like this as a child, it can strongly influence your response to criticism as an adult.

It can be helpful to realize that others in your family may have had problems themselves in relating to you, and you may not in fact have been doing anything wrong at all. Perhaps others felt more important if they could criticize you or do things for you. Perhaps they were uncertain themselves and were just trying to find a better way. If this has been your experience, remind yourself that it was not your error, that there was nothing wrong with you—it was someone else who created the problem.

You are the only one who can decide whether a problem you encounter is based on your past or whether there actually is a problem with the current situation. Generally, it's a mixture of both, and it may take some work and attention to yourself to sort out which is which. But once you can begin to clear out some of the perceptions that cling to you from the past, you'll be able to see people in the business as being part of a dynamic whole—just as you are a part of it—instead of as having more power than you do. And if you can focus on connecting with others from your heart, instead of from your past, your relationships in the business will become simpler, clearer, and more deeply fulfilling.

CHAPTER FOUR

PROMOTING YOURSELF WITHOUT LOSING YOURSELF

Marketing and promotion can be one of the biggest stumbling blocks of all for actors. Most actors choose acting because they love the art form, not because they enjoy learning about and working with business practices and ideas. Unfortunately, in the business today, an actor must be a business person first and an artist second. After all, you only get to practice the art once you've "closed the sale" by getting the job.

Creating a business plan for yourself can be an important tool in building the career you want. If you have a strong aversion to the idea of working on the business aspect, or if you have no idea how to begin, you might want to take a short general business or marketing course at a local college or school just to get some basics. This can help you to understand how the world works in terms of advertising and marketing. But if the idea of "making it a business" rather than just enjoying your art really goes against your grain, you should do some serious thinking before embarking on a career in

New York, Los Angeles, or other major cities, because your prime concern when you pursue a career in a major city will have to be the business aspect of it, probably for a very long time. If you do decide to pursue the business in a major city, remember that a good salesperson has to believe whole-heartedly that his or her product is the best, so get your product (talent and skills) in shape before you start to market yourself. Promotion will be easi-er when you're more confident about your technique.

Understanding some of your basic feelings and beliefs surrounding pro-motion and marketing can make the business aspect of your career more comfortable for you. Was there a time when someone led you to believe that if you took certain steps or followed a prescribed path they had out-lined, you'd end up getting what you wanted—and even though you fol-lowed all the instructions you still didn't get what you wanted? This is the essence of the acting business: You may do everything you possibly can to achieve success, and it still may not happen. If you come from a back-ground where most things were worked toward and achieved in an orderly, step-by-step fashion, you may have particular trouble negotiating an acting career with its extreme unpredictabilty. Most of us, taught as children that to achieve a desired result there were certain steps to take, certain paths to follow that would lead us to what we want, find out in the acting business that taking the required steps doesn't always ensure success.

You need to find ways to be creative and to express your uniqueness when you're promoting yourself. And you need to realize that the ups and downs of the business are a natural part of pursuing an acting career, and may have nothing to do with your talent, who you are, or what steps you take.

Many creative people in the arts in general feel that business is too logical, structured, or political for them to deal with. But business can be handled very creatively once you are familiar with the basic concepts of marketing. If you can approach the business with the creative part of your mind as well as with your sense of logic and business knowledge, your marketing efforts will be much more satisfying and, most likely, more successful as well. And it becomes much easier when you can clear away some of the emotional asso-ciations surrounding the idea of promoting yourself.

MODESTY IS A MARKETING NO-NO

Promoting yourself may be particularly difficult for you because of the emphasis our society has placed on modesty. You may have heard someone say, "Don't toot your own horn" and received messages, spoken or unspo-ken, that it's "not nice" to promote yourself. The problem with this is that your natural response can be to assume that someone else will promote you, that others will be quick to appreciate and compliment your talent, intelligence, inventiveness, or whatever your best qualities are. Unfortunately, this is usually not the case. Especially in the acting business, people can be busy enough or self-absorbed enough that they may not notice you unless you really do promote yourself.

As an exercise, think back to the times in your life when you did something well and felt proud of it:

- Did you receive any messages at that time that it wasn't a good idea to let other people know you were proud?

- Did people become angry or jealous of you?

- Did others put you down when you attracted attention?

Children can be very inventive in coming up with ways of doing and seeing things and they are quite often proud about it. But this can be very threatening to others in the family situation who may not be as creative or flexible, or who may have outside pressures that prevent them from appreciating those significant qualities in a child.

It's important to remind yourself that *you* can value the wonderful qualities you possess and the achievements in your life, whether or not others do the same. The issue is one of self-esteem: Do you feel that what you have to offer is important to other people? Even if others appear to think otherwise, you must believe for yourself that you do have a lot to offer. Promoting yourself, expressing pride in who you are and what you do, is a skill like any other. With a little practice, taking one step at a time, it will become easier and easier. Find ways to get support for yourself—from support groups, friends, or a good therapist, or by reading books on self-esteem. The concept of nurturing your "inner child" is explored in a number of current books (see "Recommended Reading", page 171), and these can benefit you as well. The more you can increase your self-esteem, the more you'll enjoy your life and the easier it will be to promote yourself. When you value yourself, eventually others will come to value you as well, treating you as you treat yourself. And even if some don't, you'll know it's not a reflection of who you are.

ISSUES OF SELF AND IMAGE

There can also be a problem for actors with relating the self too heavily to the "image" or "product." You may feel you always have to be on your best behavior because you never know whom you'll meet. This can be a cover-up for underlying feelings of unworthiness. You may have been taught that certain aspects of your self were not acceptable, or that when you were around other people (especially people from whom you wanted something) you had to behave in certain ways. Think about this issue for a moment: Do you feel like you're always performing or playing a role, even when you're not onstage or in front of a camera? Do you feel you always have to measure up to a certain ideal image—the way you look in your photo, a role model you've chosen, or something someone else expects of you? If you find that you're often afraid of slipping up somehow and letting something through the cracks that isn't part of the image you're promoting, you may have a problem in this area.

Some people are so fearful that their real selves are unacceptable that they may even play roles or hide themselves, even with people they are close to. They may use the role of "being an actor" to avoid being true to themselves in real life. If you find yourself wishing you could be closer to and more intimate with others, you may need to examine whether you are hiding yourself in this way. Thinking back on your life, try to recall a time when you really felt you could truthfully be yourself with someone. How did it feel? Do you feel you've moved away from that or changed in promoting yourself and your acting career?

If you have no such memory or feeling, pretend for a moment that you're three or four years old—the age when a child will speak the truth, no matter how blatant or hideous. What would that child say about the business? About whether or not you enjoy your life and your relationships? Listening to that inner child's voice can help you discover which parts of your life might be unfulfilling or painful and can be a tremendous help in changing your life so that you are happier and more fulfilled.

In recent years, show business has become more and more dependent on promoting an image rather than on talent or art. This development can deeply affect the way you see yourself simply because a major part of your identity is wrapped up in being an actor. Actors and personalities lend their faces and images to products, life-styles, and even belief systems. We don't often see the real person behind the image. Even when giving interviews, most actors and personalities are presenting a public persona that only incorporates part of their true selves, and when they appear before the public, they are usually well-polished, perfectly groomed and dressed. This can send a subliminal message that they are not real people but simply images— almost two-dimensional—even though they have fears and problems and bad days like everyone else.

These subliminal messages can also give you the feeling that you always have to look perfect or behave in a particular way, even when you're just running errands or doing laundry. It can be a burden to believe that if you aren't absolutely perfect in every way, you could lose a big opportunity. This issue can cause major dissatisfaction in your life if its roots are not uncovered, because you'll never find satisfaction if you're always striving for something that's unattainable. If you feel you're not perfect, it may make you uncomfortable with promoting yourself. Perfection is a nonproductive goal, and, in fact, a quality you see in yourself as being imperfect may be just the quirk that makes you more castable as an actor.

Learn to accept and appreciate *all* the parts of yourself—it's the combination of all the facets of your personality that makes you uniquely you.

Your Image: Is It Really You?

Because photos and résumés are such an important part of an actor's marketing program, they can hold a lot of impact in terms of your emotional response to them. When casting people receive your photo, they will judge your talents and abilities based on what the photo and résumé project. Some may take a further step and form an opinion of who you are as a person as well. Even when they see you in person at an audition or interview, they may be seeing several hundred other actors, so again they may base much of their opinion on your photo and résumé. This can make the photo and résumé seem extremely important to an actor.

However, it's essential to remember that a photo and résumé are simply marketing tools. Although they represent your look and your experience as an actor, they are not a complete representation of you as a person. There is no way that any photo and résumé can accurately convey who you are in your complexity and uniqueness as a human being, or completely indicate the depth of your talent. Photos and résumés are, practically speaking, a business card with your face on the front and your experience on the back—hardly the whole story of who you are as a person. The more clearly you can see them as tools and understand how they affect you, the more positive your relationship with the business will become.

Here again, problems can arise because the actor uses the self, rather than tools which are separate from and outside the self, as the instrument in creating art. A visual artist can market work by presenting slides of the actual work, and a musician can market a demo tape, but the marketing tool of the actor is a merely one-dimensional representation of a three-dimensional person. Its simple list of past credits gives no real demonstration of talent or ability.

Because photos and résumés are an actor's primary marketing tool, they become extremely important, and you may feel that if you can just get a great photo, you'll be on your way to success. But often, in an attempt to put as much vitality into his or her headshot as possible, an actor will try to create an idealized, perfect image in the photo. This is an instance where you may be feeling that you have to live up to a particular image or ideal. If you grew up in a family in which it was difficult to get attention, you may feel you have to look or be spectacular or perfect in order to get a response. We all have an ideal of ourselves that we'd like to live up to, but there is a difference between striving to grow toward what you believe is the best in yourself and having a fantasy-like image of yourself.

Because the world of acting is based on illusion and invention, it's tempting to present a facade, to make yourself appear in your photos as something more than or different from the real you. It's certainly a good idea to have a photo that shows you at your best, but if you choose a photo that shows an idealized image of you, it can work against you in two ways: One is that casting people may have trouble believing that such a flawless person exists; the other is that if you are successful, it will be that idealized image which creates the success, not who you really are. As the years go by, you'll always be trying to live up to that image, rather than growing as a person and as an actor.

YOUR RÉSUMÉ

Résumés are important to actors because they represent the sum total of their experience and training—the story of each actor's life as an actor. Along with your experience and training, your résumé may also represent to you your unconscious, deep-seated feelings about yourself and your value as a person. When actors are first starting out in the business, they sometimes feel they need to pad their résumés to make it seem as if they have more experience than they actually do. This is a mistake, not only because it's fairly easy to get caught in a lie, but also because if you are hired partly on the basis of your inflated experience, you may end up losing the job because you don't have the experience and ability you professed to have. Everyone has to start somewhere—even actors who are major stars today had only one or two credits on their résumés at some point.

Part of the problem may be the opinion in our society that if you're not already "there," you're never going to make it. Many people are extremely achievement-oriented, and the pervasiveness of this attitude can lead us to believe that we're not good enough as we are, that we have to pretend to be better or further along in order to be worthy in the eyes of ourselves and others. Working for achievement is not a bad thing in itself; it's only when you feel you're unworthy unless you're already achieving your highest dreams that you get into trouble.

If you don't have as much experience as you'd like, or haven't worked on as high a level as you'd like, there's no need to hide the fact. People know they can trust those who tell the truth to have integrity in other areas, and this is true in the business as well. As soon as you feel you have to hide something or be someone you're not, you lose a part of yourself to the marketing process; it becomes much harder to believe in yourself and to stay centered and relaxed when you're interacting with others.

You'll get more satisfaction out of your work if your perspective on performing is that you're learning about yourself and the world, deepening your talent, and working on your craft, rather than just adding another credit to your résumé. If you're doing the work mostly for the credits, mostly to try to get up to the next rung of the ladder, you'll never find satisfaction, because there are always more steps to take, more choices to make—there's always further to go. There will never come a time when you're finally set, in any area of life, so it's best to ease away from a single goal of achievement and let yourself enjoy the process of building your career and growing as an actor. Learn to feel more comfortable with where you already are and who you are right now.

Life can be a wonderful teacher and a glorious exploration if you let it unfold in a natural way, rather than trying to control it or attempting to be someone you're not.

YOUR PHOTO

It's important to get a photo that you really love—one that shows the best that you believe is in you, the qualities that make you different from everyone else. It can be helpful to get feedback from people in the business as to what constitutes a good photo, but, again, everyone's perspective is different, and you are the one who must mail your photo time after time and hand it to casting people. You may need to keep trying until you get a photo that pleases you all over again each time you give it to someone, but that's much better than having a photo that someone else may have liked, but that you're not sure of. If you're unsure whether you like the photo, you'll feel unsure of yourself every time you mail it or hand it out.

One problem with using a photo you're unsure of is that if you do feel you should "match up" with the photo when you go to an audition, you may close off the best parts of yourself (hiding what the photo doesn't show) or feel that you're being phony. For example, if the photo is a "glamour shot," every time you go to an audition you'll feel a need to be your most glamorous self. This can be difficult on bad days—we all have those. Or, if you're not up to matching the photo, you may look different enough from it to annoy the casting person and thus lose the opportunity you worked so hard for.

Before you select a shot from the contact sheet your photographer has sent you, it doesn't hurt to get responses from a number of people as to which photos appeal to them. But remember that friends may perceive you in a certain way, and this can influence what they see or don't see in your photos. The same goes with people in the business: If a certain agent is used to seeing you as an ingenue, and you know in your heart that it's time to move on to character or leading roles, that agent's advice may not be helpful.

On the other hand, showing your contact sheets to others can be very helpful in terms of finding out if there is a discrepancy between the way others see you and how you see yourself. In choosing a photo, keep in mind that if everyone else thinks the photo you would choose doesn't look like the real you, you may be trying to project an image that is wrong for you. But it's most important that you are comfortable with the photo and that you feel it represents you well. Otherwise, it will be difficult for you to mail it out; you'll never be satisfied with your current photo, and you'll always be wanting to get a new one.

The best approach is to listen to others' opinions, take what's important to you and leave the rest, and then trust your own feelings so that you will end up with a photo that excites you, that you feel projects the essential you. It may seem difficult at first to trust your own instincts, but the more you learn to, the stronger and more sure they will grow.

"Am I Just a Type?"

When you're getting photos done, try as much as possible to get a photo that shows you as an individual rather than as a particular type. It's certainly fine to dress like a "young mom," for instance, if that's what you play best, but if you don't enjoy children and wouldn't be interested in being a mom in real life, the discrepancy will probably come through, either in your photos or when you meet casting people in person. This can be confusing to them when they see you. As you work to get to know your-self better and begin to learn what qualities are special to you, let your photo reflect your strengths and weaknesses—whatever sets you apart from other actors.

The danger in seeing yourself as a type is that there are always a number of other actors who are the same type. You may begin unconsciously to believe that you are only one among many of the same kind of person, replaceable by anyone else, a dime a dozen. It may seem incredible that feel-ings like these can arise, but over time a constant message such as this can work its way into the unconcious, causing resentment and bitterness.

Trying to fit yourself into a type can make your photo look like a num-ber of others of the same type that cross the casting person's desk, instead of standing out from the rest. Even though you may, as a performer, fit into the same type or range that a lot of other actors do, what will make you stand out is your uniqueness. If you feel that you must present yourself as a type in your photo, try to lend your personal style to it—don't erase your uniqueness in fitting yourself to the type. Casting people often don't know exactly what they're looking for until they see it, and sometimes it's the actor who is a little "off type" that makes them sit up and take notice.

Whether you choose to go with or against type in your photos, remem-ber that the "product" you're presenting in the photo is only a part of you, just as your acting career is only one facet of your life. You are not marketing your self—your feelings, experiences, and attitudes—you are marketing skills and talents that are only a part of your complex and unique individuality.

The tendency of the industry itself to typecast people can compound the problem of confusing your self with your image. Making yourself conform to a certain type can be a direct reflection of roles you may have had to play in your family, and consequently you may not be acknowledging some facets of yourself. The most obvious example of this is people who were brought up to be "nice," rather than creative or effective or even simply human beings. You may want to do some thinking about whether the types you may have considered for yourself are based on roles you felt you had to play in childhood.

When a child is born into a family, the family system of relationships is already set up, and the child may be subtly or overtly pushed into playing a particular role. One child may "act out" some of the fear or anger that oth-ers in the family have difficulty expressing and become the scapegoat or the rebel in the family; another may become the "good child" in order to get attention or to maintain the family's dignity if there are problems. If one type in the business seems more comfortable and familiar to you than others, or if you become frustrated or uncomfortable when people suggest that you are a particular type, you may be reacting to feelings about your own role in your family system.

Think back again to your early years and consider these questions:

- Did you feel you had to play a particular role or behave a certain way in order to feel part of the family, to be accepted, or even to survive?

- Did you try to make up for the problems in your family or to "fix" things that seemed unbalanced?

- Did you feel you were the only one who did everything wrong, who caused all the problems, even though you were just trying to express yourself?

Family roles can be very powerful influences, even when you have become an adult, and the industry's tendency to typecast can revive or aggravate early patterns of role-playing. The more you can delve into the ways your past roles influence your present life, and the type you (or others) think you fit into, the more you'll discover who you really are underneath the imposed roles from your past.

Also spend some time thinking about the different roles played by members of your family and the ways in which each person's relationships with other family members affected the whole:

- Who was in charge and why?

- Who cleaned up the "messes" (literally and figuratively) that others made?

- How did you feel about your parents when you were small?

- How did they respond to you—as an individual, or as a sort of "cog in the wheel" in the family?

- Was the way they responded to you different from the way they responded to other children?

- Was your behavior accepted when you stepped outside of your "role"?

Family roles are usually thrust upon a child at a very early age, and for this reason it can be difficult to uncover the patterns and move beyond them.

This issue deserves as much attention as you can give it. Be alert in your day-to-day life to the ways your family role and how you might be "typed" affect your behavior in the business, in relationships, and on the job.

Look for opportunities to express aspects of yourself that are different from your family role and your type and let yourself discover the numerous facets of yourself as an individual. Bring as much of yourself into your professional image as you can, rather than trying to cut away or mask certain parts of yourself in order to fit into a category. Treat every aspect of your personality with respect—each is a part of you that deserves expression. When a new feeling or attitude arises within you, allow it into your life as much as you can.

Discover your unusual aspects as much as you can, find ways to fan the flame inside you that strives to be different, and try to magnify for yourself the unique essence of your personality. This is what casting people are looking for: who you are, and how you express your individuality and humanity.

DIRECT MARKETING: ACTORS' MAILINGS

One of the most difficult and disappointing aspects of the business can be the lack of response that most actors experience after mailing out their photo–résumés. You can send out a hundred of these and get perhaps only a few responses, or none at all. If this aspect of the business bothers you, or if you find yourself giving up after only a few tries, you may have a history of feeling that others weren't responding to you in the way you wanted.

Think back again to your family: Was there a person, or people, whom you really wanted to reach with your deepest self, to connect with, to get a genuine response from? Did you have to struggle to get others to pay attention to you? This can be both an intense and delicate issue, so treat your feelings here with the deepest respect and care.

Many of us, as children, weren't given the love and attention we wanted and needed on a day-to-day basis. When you were young, there may not have been much concern about whether your needs were met or not—perhaps there were pressing concerns in other areas for the adults in your family, causing them to be inattentive or unresponsive toward you. What is important is to realize that you are *worthy* of attention and always have been, whether you got it or not.

If you can separate your mailing tasks from old feelings about not getting the responses you wanted, those tasks will be much easier to do. You'll know that it's most likely just the sheer volume of photo–résumés that peo-ple receive that causes the lack of response, rather than any shortcomings on your part.

Any work you can do on a lack-of-response problem will help you feel more comfortable with promoting yourself and will also help lessen the pain of rejection. Begin to notice the times in your life when people do respond well to you—when friends laugh at your jokes and enjoy your com-pany, when fellow workers appreciate your efforts, or when someone says, "Hey, that's a great idea!" Often we tend to overlook the positive things that others say about us and become obsessed with the negative. It's usually eas-ier to give in and listen to negative voices from the past than to choose to override them and create something better. Even if those good moments seem few and far between, the more you focus on them, the more you'll notice that people in your life do respond to you. They perhaps do not always do so in exactly the way you'd like, but the more you focus on the responses that make you feel good, the more of them you'll find. The important thing to remember here is not that other people's treatment of you is more significant than your own feelings and opinions, but that you actually deserve and get their response.

If one of your biggest problems is getting motivated to send out your mailings, you're not alone. Many actors have trouble with this. Although part of the problem may be that sending photos is related to business and marketing, it may also have to do with the fact that we were told what to do when we were children and didn't like it. First in the family and then for a number of years in school, you were expected to do what you "should" do—household chores, homework, and so on—and now, even though you're an adult, you may feel like someone is telling you what to do all over again.

Check your feelings here: When you're having trouble doing mailings, do you feel you want to avoid it because it's hard to push yourself out there over and over again, or do you feel as if someone is telling you that you should send out your photos if you want to be an actor? Mailings can be an important part of building an acting career, but if you're feeling like you're doing them only because someone said you should, it's naturally discouraging.

Much of the time when we were young, what parents and teachers told us we should do was for them, or to help us achieve something they thought we should achieve, rather than for our own best interests. And when we become adults, it's easy to feel that anything we try to accomplish is for someone else as well. We may continue to look to others in hopes of getting some direction and follow others' suggestions rather than creating new methods to get what we want.

Try to keep reminding yourself that sending photos is a choice that you make in the present so that you can build a career, not something you're doing because, as in your childhood, someone "said so."

Be creative—there are a number of ways to promote yourself as an actor, and sending photos is only one of the options. Spend some time thinking about other ways to promote yourself besides just mailing photos. Consider producing a show with other actors or a one-person show for yourself.

Finding a Better Perspective

Actors can also make a major mistake in thinking that if they've been working at the business for a long time, even years, without getting a real response, they must not be good enough. This too can deflate self-esteem over a period of time. Even if you're extremely talented, it takes a long, long time to build a career; it can take anywhere from five to twenty-five years to build a network that allows you to work fairly regularly. And even extremely talented actors don't always make it, for any number of possible reasons. You need to learn to leave each audition behind when it's over. If you always expect a response, or if you hope that each audition will be "the one" that will set you on the road to stardom, you'll be constantly disappointed, and it will get harder and harder to keep working at the business. Instead, think of each audition as a small step, as a building block, in the process of creating the career you want. And remember that it is a process—the journey is more important than the end result. A successful career usually comes out of a process of taking one step at a time, then the next, and creating and building on each step as you go, rather than catching a single lucky break.

If you are pursuing an acting career because your dream is to become a star, you may have an unrealistic view of yourself and the business that will only weigh you down in your self-promotion efforts. It might be helpful to look more closely at this dream career you aspire to have and examine your motives. If you believe that becoming a star will give you power and confidence and meet your emotional needs, you should realize that being a star, in itself, would not help you achieve that. Stars are generally no more happy or successful in their personal lives than other people. Trying to make a dream of stardom come true has led many an actor to lose him- or herself by going to great lengths to "make it." In most cases the extremes they went to only served to take their focus off of their real lives and robbed them of chances to create happy and fulfilling lives for themselves in and out of the business. If your present life—or the way your career is going—is not bringing you the happiness you desire, you need to discover exactly what it is you would enjoy about being a successful actor and find other ways to meet those needs in your life (see Chapter 5 and Exercises). With more realistic expectations, you will relieve yourself of an overburdened and unsatisfying journey through your performing career.

Of course, it's important to discover for yourself exactly where you want your career to lead so that you will choose the best way to promote yourself. There are so many possibilities open to actors—in theater, film, television, industrials, commercials, student films, nonbroadcast media, and so on—that it's best to concentrate on one or two areas, at least at first. One way to discover what your goals are is to think of what you want in present terms: "I am performing in a Shakespeare play Off-Broadway." Those who work with affirmations stress the importance of phrasing them in the present tense: "I am very successful, and I enjoy my success." If you envision the things you'd like to do and have as being in the distant future, they will remain, always, in the distant future. So begin to create what you want in terms of the present.

One helpful aspect of this kind of "present-time thinking" is that, if you are truthful with yourself, you will often discover how you really feel about what you think you want. For instance, if you are thinking, "I am doing *Julius Caesar* Off-Broadway," you might notice that certain feelings arise, and these can be clues which will lead you in the direction you need to go. If the idea of doing Shakespeare's play Off-Broadway creates a lot of anxiety for you, this might be a sign that you're not ready to work on that level, that you need to pursue work which would eventually lead to that, rather than trying to jump off the cliff all at once.

On the other hand, if *Julius Caesar* suddenly seems less daring than the performance-art piece you auditioned for last week, you'll understand your feelings and desires in a different way. The key is to imagine yourself already in a particular situation, and then you'll discover how you really feel about it. Deal with your feelings immediately and directly, whenever possible; if you deny them, feelings will pile up in your unconscious and can undermine your life and your work.

The more you can target the areas of the business you're particularly interested in and the more specifically you can tailor your marketing plan, the less time you'll spend going to auditions that waste your time. Many actors try to go to every possible audition, but if you choose just one or two areas that excite you, you'll have more time and energy available to focus on promoting yourself as a distinct individual. Spend as much time as you can getting clear about what you want from your career. It can be very easy to get distracted or overwhelmed because there are so many areas to focus on—and then there are the myriad differing opinions you'll get from everyone else as to where you fit in. Only you can know everything there is to know about yourself, and only you can know what you really want out of your career and your life. The clearer you become about your goal, the easier it will become for you to find ways to attain it.

PRESENTING YOURSELF AS A LEADING PERFORMER

Through the years, a lot of confusion has developed concerning the nature of a leading man or woman. The line separating roles and performers has become blurred, and the idea of stardom and celebrity has rendered the categories even more indistinct. In the past, a leading actor was one who had a lot of experience, was at the head of the cast, and had the largest or most important role in the show. Any actor is more likely to succeed if he or she can project a sureness of self, but leading performers, in particular, need to exude self-esteem and charisma. It's very important, if you choose to present yourself as a leading performer, that you work especially hard on your self-esteem. When casting people need to fill a show's major role, they look for someone with the confidence and magnetism of a leader. If you try to fit yourself into this category at the beginning of your career, you can undermine your efforts early on. It's better to "play the field" awhile, develop your uniqueness, and discover for yourself whether or not you actually enjoy being a leader. If it's who you really are, if it's part of your essence (or a part of yourself you'd like to develop), then gather your courage and make the leap.

Leading actors are generally cast as characters who can accomplish most tasks that are set before them, often characters we believe could survive on their own in the jungle or the desert, or lead others to a better life—in short, characters with exceptional abilities, intelligence, and stamina. If you attempt to market yourself as a leading person, but don't feel deep inside that you could rise to the occasion if circumstances called for a leader, you may undermine your self-esteem, and cause yourself unnecessary fear and doubt. It's best to wait and to gain experience until you have the confidence to promote yourself as a leading performer. It can be a tremendous task to become one, and it will probably take many years to build your career up to this level. Remember also that as overcrowded as the business is in general, very few people make it as leading performers. Most actors who work on a regular basis are acting in supporting or smaller character roles.

In fact, character roles can offer exciting opportunities to use your imagination and broaden your talent, and choosing to pursue work as a character actor can lead you to a depth in your acting work that you might not find as a leading performer.

Promoting yourself may not be your favorite part of building an acting career, but if you can remove some of the emotional baggage surrounding it and discover exactly what it is that you want to achieve in the business, you'll find it much easier to promote yourself without losing yourself, and you will most likely be more successful as well.

CHAPTER FIVE

GETTING A LIFE OUTSIDE THE BUSINESS

Pursuing a performing career can require immense amounts of time and energy from actors: mailing photo–résumés and flyers, taking classes, interviewing, going to auditions, and performing in shows or films. If you're not paying attention, you may suddenly realize one day that it has completely taken over your life and become your entire focus. There are many reasons to "get a life" outside the business: for variety, to get a wider perspective on life, and to have other interests when business is slow. Most importantly, you might as well enjoy some of your life instead of spending every minute looking for a job. It's easy to get so wrapped up in trying to make it as an actor that you may find you're perceiving yourself *only* as an actor who is trying to make it instead of as a person with a varied and fulfilling life—something the pursuit of a career as an actor is only part of.

THE SEARCH FOR EXCITEMENT

Acting can be a mood-altering activity, a "high" that seems to make the rest of your life more bearable. If your foremost self-identity is "I am an actor," that may mean you see yourself as a creative, spontaneous, vital being *because* you are an actor, instead of seeing yourself as having those qualities because you are who you are. Needing to identify yourself as an actor can be a cover-up for feelings of worthlessness as a person (which almost everyone has to some degree). Our cultural beliefs include the idea that actors lead very exciting lives—traveling to this or that locale to do a film, giving interviews, possibly jaunting back and forth between homes in the city and country. If this is part of what you seek as an actor, you may end up being disappointed if your career doesn't build the way you want it to. If you expect that the excitement you want in your life will come only from being an actor, you may be missing out on creating an exciting life for yourself as a person outside the business.

Part of the attraction of acting for you may be that characters on the stage and screen usually live intense, dramatic lives. If you felt stifled as a child or were taught to fear the new and exciting, you may be inordinately drawn to the stimulus of living through a character's story to enjoy the richness and diversity of human experience, rather than embracing real life as fully as you can. The world of show business can look very glamorous to someone who was raised in a rather colorless atmosphere or to someone who had a very strict or religious upbringing. Therefore the primary appeal of show business for some actors may be the prospect of working with other talented people, possibly even having a relationship with a person who is attractive, charming, and passionate, and being immersed in a fantasy-filled world of excitement. But, of course, even an actor who is working steadily in the business may not succeed in satisfying these desires.

One of the ways you can work toward greater fulfillment in your life is to explore outside the business for other things life has to offer. Make it a point to build or maintain a healthy interest in other areas besides acting and the business: Visit museums or art shows; read sections of the newspaper besides the arts or theater sections; investigate free or low-cost lectures, seminars, or classes. It's easy to get so caught up in the business that you forget there are many other valuable life experiences. Meanwhile, everything you learn can help you become more diversified, so that you have more to bring to your acting work.

It's also important to have friends and associates outside the business. It can be extremely helpful to have a supportive network of friends who are actors, who know firsthand what it's like to pursue a performing career and who love acting as much as you do. Yet if *all* your relationships are based on the business, then your perspective on it—and your perspective on life as a whole—can become very narrow. This in turn can cause you to focus on the business even more in an attempt to find stimulation and fulfillment. Over time, you may put yourself in a vicious circle in which you believe that becoming a success as an actor is the only thing that could possibly make you happy. So make a point of making and nurturing relationships with people who are not involved in the business. This will help you to maintain a balanced perspective concerning your life as a whole.

THE WORLD OF PRETEND

The world of illusion that is the basis of film and theater can also be attractive because it is safe and familiar, like the "let's-pretend-there's-nothing-wrong" atmosphere within some troubled families. You may need to confront the following questions:

• Did you feel, when you were growing up, that things weren't always what they seemed?

• Did you strongly prefer the world of fantasy to real life?

• Were there certain things under the surface that you knew you weren't supposed to talk about?

• Did you feel you were part of something that seemed unreal or unnatural, as if you were somehow outside of what was going on in the real world?

These kinds of feelings can be hard to pin down, but if you think back to what life felt like for you then, compared to how it feels now, you may gain some insight into the patterns that were in place in your family.

Acting can be a beckoning world to an adventurous spirit. If as a child you wanted to be an adventurer or explorer, perhaps you've become an actor instead so that you can explore in the safer world of illusion that is acting. There may have been something you wanted for yourself when you grew up but were afraid to pursue, or were told you couldn't achieve or were better off not even trying to achieve. Family beliefs involving fear can be particularly powerful. Parents often try to keep children safe from harm by discouraging their instincts to explore. (They may themselves have a fear of new experiences.) Acting appears to offer the adventurous child a safe way to express itself. But as adventures go, an acting career, with its seesaw nature and its risks, can be frustrating and debilitating. There are many ways besides acting to find adventures in your life. Imagine for a moment that there are no such things as actors: What would you be doing instead? How would you be living your life? Would you indeed be adventurous—a traveler or explorer? Spend some time using your imagination to discover for yourself the life you'd be living if you weren't an actor. And don't be afraid of exploration: Give your attention to new things, and let the child within you explore to your heart's desire. (As an adult, you now have no one to hold you back, as you did when you were small.) What, beyond acting, attracts you?

Acting, and being an actor, are also acceptable outlets for imagination in our society. Sometimes, as a child, you may not have been allowed to express imaginative ideas, particularly if your family environment was very strict or rationality-oriented. An active imagination is, of course, an excellent tool for an actor to possess. The need to express yourself through your imagination may have been one of the reasons you chose acting in the first place, but if you don't get much chance to work as an actor, this valuable part of you may be denied expression. Imagination is a powerful tool you can utilize in other ways besides acting to create a better and more fulfilling life for yourself, to envision a better future, and to bring new ideas and possibilities into existence. You may want to explore other possible outlets for your imagination: journal writing, visualization, decorating your living space. Finger painting, in particular, can be a very satisfying way to release the imagination.

THE FALSE SELF
One of the methods children use to keep their inner selves safe and intact in a difficult environment is to create what psychologists call a *false self*: that is, parts of the self that seem to be unacceptable to the family are "split off" or covered over in order to conform to the demands of the family system. What can happen for actors from such backgrounds is that all those "unacceptable" qualities can get funneled into their acting, instead of becoming integrated into their lives as they become adults. Anger, fear, vulnerability, strength—any emotion or quality can be perceived as unacceptable within the family, depending on its beliefs. At an early age, you may have rejected certain parts of yourself; when they began to demand expression as you grew up, you may have funneled them into your acting. The danger here is that if you aren't working a lot as an actor, you aren't getting much of a chance to express those qualities. You may consequently feel a division between the parts of yourself you can express as an actor and your life as a person.

Ask yourself: Does pursuing your career—or does the possibility of getting a role—seem larger or much more important than the rest of your life?

This may be a signal that you're trying to live your life through your acting and your interaction with the business, rather than approaching your life and the business in a realistic way. If pursuing an acting career is the most important thing in your life, then you are letting the vicissitudes of the business control your life. This can lead to feelings of helplessness, feeling less able to direct your life and make of it what you want. If acting is the single most important element in your life, you may find you don't have much of a life to go back to, if you decide one day to leave the business.

A passion for acting can be, deep down, simply a passion for expressing yourself, and when you confine that passion to acting, you are using only a small amount of your infinite capacity for self-expression, especially if you don't work as often as you wish. Many people in the present time are seeking a deeper spirituality, a deeper meaning for their lives, and acting can be one of the most spiritual activities of all, in terms of self-expression, depth of understanding, and connection to others. But the business does not usually support the individual actor's search for self and meaning.

The fact that you have chosen to be an actor suggests that you are on a quest for self-understanding and deeper meaning in your life. As we have seen, acting provides a way to try out different personalities and behaviors in a safe setting, to explore the depths of yourself. Pursuing an acting career provides an unparalleled opportunity to get a feel for a variety of occupations and styles of living. If your personal interests or your desire to explore were frowned upon or discouraged at a young age, you may have chosen acting partly as a means to discover what you enjoy, who you are, and how you'd like to live your life. If this is the case for you, be wary of letting yourself get into that vicious circle in which you rely more and more on acting to provide stimulating experiences in your life and spend less and less creative energy building a life you love outside the business. Try to find other areas of your life in which you can pursue your quest for deeper meaning, excitement, and self-understanding: in work, in relationships, in other artistic pursuits, in your individual search for your own spirituality.

If something outside of the business, or some other area of the business, piques your interest, give it a try. If you've always wanted to dance the tango or learn woodcarving, take a class or find a teacher. Not only will you grow as a person (and thus as an actor), but you may eventually find something besides show business that you want to devote yourself to. At the very least, you'll be opening up new possibilities in your life for self-expression and enjoyment. You may find that when you pursue possibilities besides acting, you discover new facets of yourself and that, free for a time from auditioning for a job and being judged, you can relax and have fun.

Find ways to create a rhythm in your daily life that can further your quest for self and meaning. Once you turn some of your creative energy toward your life, instead of just focusing on your career, it will open up in ways you never imagined.

THE COMPULSION TO PERFORM

Your image of yourself as an actor may have begun in childhood and may not even necessarily be related to the enjoyment of acting. Your parents may have encouraged or demanded that you "perform" in any number of ways: grades, chores, recitals, or even just being polite when meeting their friends. Check your past:

• Did you feel that you had to "do something," or behave in a certain way, in order to be worthwhile in their eyes or to get their attention?

• Were the things that you did—your accomplishments and achieve-ments—seemingly more important to them than who you were inside, or what you thought and felt?

• When you get onstage, are you concentrating more on what others will think than on whether or not you're enjoying what you're doing?

You may be pursuing acting as a career with an unconcious hope that if you can reach some pinnacle of success (which may not even be attainable), you'll finally escape the necessity of pleasing or satisfying others and be free to express yourself as you wish. This is an extremely important area to explore: Many children are encouraged by their parents to "make us proud," and parents sometimes try to make children over in their own image, to create in their children the lives they wish they themselves had lived. This pattern can strongly affect the amount of happiness you find in your life, because if, instead of living to express your own choices and desires, you are living your life unconciously as a reaction against your par-ents' expectations—or in order to fulfill them—your life will probably be unfulfilling for you. Listen closely to your feelings and focus on whether you're doing what you want to do, or whether you feel somehow "pushed" to make certain choices. You are the only one who can discover what you want and make it happen. And if you're not living the life that you want to live, you have every right to explore other possibilities, to change your life in whatever way you want, and to make it completely your own.

If members of your family tended to suppress their emotions, or if there were problems in the family that generated tension, you may have been attracted to acting partly because the "dramatic tension" in theater and film feels familiar to you, perhaps even comfortable and safe.

- Do you recall a general feeling of tension when you were a child, or an atmosphere of combined fear and excitement?

- Was there an aura of "drama" in your family?

- Were others in your family often anxious or in conflict?

If you grew up with these feelings, finding them again (in acting or in anything else—relationships, work, and so on) can make you feel almost like you're "coming home." Try to separate what it is that you truly love and enjoy about acting from what makes you feel *compelled* to do it. A feeling of compulsion may be deeply related to working out patterns in your upbringing and is worth detailed examination. Even the difficulty that exists in building a career in demanding cities like New York or Los Angeles may represent how hard it was for you to express your feelings as a child, or how difficult it was to show your inner self to others and get a response from them.

It's vital that you begin to make your own life more important than your acting career. Even if you feel you were put on this earth to be an actor, even if the drive is so strong that you feel called to do it, you are still a human being first and an actor second. Acting is something that you can choose to do or not; it's an individual choice that you may want to devote your time to. But on a very basic level, living your life is what you're here for. Self-exploration and self-expression are at the very roots of human existence, and you need to discover yourself through the experience of living your life and creating what you want, not just through your acting. Once you make your life more important than your career, you'll begin to discover new facets of yourself and be able to bring more of yourself to any work you do, acting included.

HOW TO PUT THE LIFE BACK INTO YOUR LIFE

If you have been focusing single-mindedly on your career for a long time, it may seem odd to think about the possibility of expanding other areas of your life in order to meet some of your needs. But one way to increase your happiness and renew your energy without having to rely on the possibility of career success is to rediscover things you loved to do in your early life.

Think back to your childhood pleasures: Was there anything you enjoyed doing that you haven't even thought about for years? Did you love to paint, or to build objects with plaster of Paris? Then get some paint or plaster, and renew those feelings of enjoyment!

As adults, we often become so concerned with achieving in a particular area that we forget there are other things which also give us pleasure—and which we can enjoy without trying to "get somewhere." You don't have to change careers and become a painter or musician to be engaged in other arts; they can provide you with something to do just for the joy of it, unconcerned with the result. You may discover things about yourself you never knew or had forgotten, and most likely you'll rekindle some of your zest for life. And having other choices as to how you can imaginatively express your thoughts and feelings can ease the pressure you feel to be a success as an actor.

Spend some time thinking about other areas of your life as well. If there is a particular aspect of your life outside the business that is unsatisfying to you, or if most of it is, you'll be well rewarded by any time and energy you spend in thinking about how you can change it for the better and in working to create something that is more satisfying and fulfilling for you. It can seem difficult to make changes in terms of jobs, relationships, or living situations, but it will probably be easier than you think, once you make the decision to have a better quality of life. Take the steps one at a time, ask for help if you need it, and remind yourself that you are the one who's in charge of your life now. You have the power to create a life that offers as much variety, enjoyment, and fulfillment as you want, whether or not your career turns out the way you expect.

CHAPTER SIX

ROLE-PLAYING: A SUBSTITUTE FOR LIVING YOUR LIFE

One of the primary explanations actors give for their passion for acting is the opportunity to play a variety of roles, from murderers to saints, hillbillies to sophisticates. What is it that you really enjoy about playing different roles? Perhaps one of the things you love about acting is that you get to explore previously unexpressed parts of yourself—your anger, or cleverness, or even some aspect of your sexuality. Acting may have become a way for you to express parts of yourself that you were taught were inappropriate in life. Do some thinking about the past:

- What were the roles you were encouraged to enact in your family?

- Were you the "rebel," or the "good" child? What label would you put on your role?

- Were there certain emotions or qualities you weren't allowed to express, or that you never saw others in your family express?

- Did you feel you had to hide certain parts of yourself?

Examination in this area can help to clarify why you chose to be an actor, and what you're truly seeking in terms of your career. Especially note any differences between what you're feeling inside when you're alone, and the way you express yourself when you're with other people.

One way to discover whether or not there are differences between the inner person you really are and the face you present to the world is to consider the roles you've been cast in. If you've always wanted to play Lady Macbeth but you're always cast as Viola, there may be a discrepancy between what you feel inside and want to express and the outer self you let others see. It can be tiring and uncomfortable after a while to live a double life in this way, and sometimes it's difficult to keep or even develop a strong sense of self if you're constantly feeling one way, yet expressing yourself in another. It may help to recognize that all emotions are a part of every one of us; what makes us individual is the combination of feelings, beliefs, and attitudes. Everyone gets angry at certain things, and everyone is sad sometimes—this is a natural part of being human. If you find that you aren't experiencing these emotions spontaneously from time to time, you may be relying on acting to express facets of yourself that you've been unwilling to face.

YOUR DREAM ROLE: THE REAL YOU?

Consider the roles you've always wanted to play—Hamlet, or Cleopatra, or your own dream role:

• What is it, exactly, that fascinates you? What facets of the character particularly draw you?

• Do you think you would enjoy living that character's life, being that person? If so, why?

• How would it be different from the way you feel you respond to life?

• What qualities would you like to bring into your real life, to learn to express, while playing that role?

A strong desire to do a particular role can represent aspects of yourself that you want to learn to express. It's naturally safer to learn to do that in a role, where the emotions you're expressing are part of the world of pretend, the responses to your actions are pretty much predictable, and you're not personally responsible to others for your behavior as the character. But if this is the case and you *don't* get to play that role, then you may never get to discover fully those aspects of yourself that are related to the role.

Try imagining the character you'd like to play as a part of yourself. (After all, you would bring out certain qualities in yourself to create that character if you did play the role.) What are the qualities of your favorite character—vitality, sexuality, vulnerability, strength—that particularly excite you? How would your own life be different if those qualities were a prominent part of who you are? These qualities may represent aspects of yourself that you'd like to develop and deepen. Explore these areas as much as you can. If you're stuck concerning a decision or a specific situation, ask yourself what your favorite character would do, and then examine your emotional reaction—is that something you would consider doing as well? If not, why not?

This is not to say that you should be playing a character or acting a role in real life. It is, or should be, more enjoyable to be yourself, with your own innumerable qualities and infinite freedom of choice. But the qualities that attract you to a favorite character are qualities you already possess, even if you've never expressed them. Because that character you especially love often represents some unexpressed wish or undiscovered feeling in real life, you need to identify those attractive qualities and discover ways to express them in your day-to-day life—not just in your acting.

It's important to acknowledge every aspect of yourself. It's no sin to want to be a king or a queen, a business tycoon, a star athlete, a sexy or strong or vulnerable person. In fact, those aspects of yourself that urge you to grow, to become more tomorrow than you are today, are qualities of yourself that you should treasure and appreciate—they can lead you to a deeper enjoyment of your life. The problem is that if these desires aren't satisfied, either through acting or some other pursuit, they can become part of the "shadow," or dark side, of your unconcious mind and cause problems in your daily life, rather than becoming integrated parts of your personality.

If acting is truly the only way you have to express your emotions, then as long as you are between jobs you are, in essence, waiting for someone else's permission to express yourself. Not getting this permission, you may find yourself very frustrated, or you may become highly reactive and emotional at times, unable to find balance in your responses to people and events. If this happens to you, it can be an excellent opportunity to look at your needs and feelings outside the business. Ask yourself why a particular person or situation is causing you to be emotional. Are your feelings really warranted in terms of your life as a whole? Worrying, getting "stressed out" or excessively emotional rarely solves a problem. Mostly these responses waste energy that could be put to better use; they distract you from more important pursuits. Try to sort out the important issues from the trivial ones. If a given situation is very important to you, your feelings are probably justified. But if you find yourself becoming too emotional over little things that would not bother you if you were working on a role, then dealing with your emotions outside of acting may indeed be a problem you should work on.

ACTORS AND EMOTIONS

You may have unconsciously chosen acting as a profession because of an underlying need to sort through and untangle your emotions. In the family setting, emotions can become confused and entangled, and if the family is a very troubled one, or if a child is very sensitive, this jumble of emotions can be overwhelming. As the child becomes an adult, the accumulation of these confused feelings over time cannot be sorted and understood without some form of structure. Acting can provide such a structure, allowing the actor to be one character, then another, experiencing one sequence of emotions, then another, until the jumble of feelings can be uncovered, sorted, and understood.

If you learned or were forced to bottle up your feelings when you were small, it probably became a habit for you, and you may have unconsciously chosen acting as a way to release pent-up emotions. The problem with this is twofold: First, if you are using your pent-up emotions to create a character, the character can end up appearing one-sided or overblown, depending on which emotion(s) you most need to release. Second, if you are not getting roles or finding some way to explore these facets of yourself, your feelings will continue to be bottled up and entangled.

One underlying reason many people choose acting is to gain experience in expressing powerful emotions in a safe and regulated atmosphere. If you were to fly into a rage in real life, you might fear the consequences, thinking that you could harm yourself or someone else. Actually, the same part of you that "watches" when you're onstage—so that you can remember lines and blocking and stay on the path you've set for yourself—is also present when you are experiencing strong emotions in real life. But if your emotions have been bottled up for a long time, you may feel as if you're going to explode when you're angry or cry forever when you're sad. It can help to remind yourself that the process of expressing emotions, even very deep and powerful ones, is quite natural (babies do it very easily) and is naturally regulated by the mind–body system. A point generally comes when you have expressed what you needed to express or have exhausted the feelings, and they subside.

If you are not used to looking at and dealing with your feelings outside of acting, the prospect can seem overwhelming at first. But mastering response patterns that are rooted in your past will make the business easier for you, and your need for self-expression will no longer be frustrated when you're not acting.

Many actors are somewhat shy when they're offstage, and this is the other side of the coin: If you rely on acting as an outlet for self-expression, it can become more and more difficult to express yourself in day-to-day life. It's important to begin connecting with your feelings at a pace that is comfortable for you, to help you feel as safe with genuine self-expression as you feel with expressing yourself through acting. Start by setting aside just 5 or 10 minutes a day to sit down with yourself. Examine how you feel about what's going on in your life. Often we get so caught up in getting everything done, or trying to move forward, that we don't pay attention to what we're really feeling inside. Having too much to do can actually be a way of running away from feelings that we're afraid of facing.

When you give attention to your feelings and discover a feeling that's different from what you've experienced before, explore it as much as you can. Feelings that are not what you're used to can lead to new areas of growth and understanding. As you learn to listen to your feelings, remember to treat yourself with respect and gentleness, for feelings can be delicate. Moreover, they are always there for a reason—as a response to a current situation, or as a reappearance of past emotions which need to be released. Your feelings are good allies: They can warn you of dangerous or hurtful situations, and they can help you create the life you want.

The Feeling of Being Special

Another reason that acting attracts certain people is that it satisfies their need to feel special. Many people were not given the attention and respect they deserved when they were small, and this resulted in a strong need for attention as an adult. When you're onstage or in front of a camera, you're getting attention. In fact, the audience in a theater has paid to give you their attention, and the crew on a film set is giving you help so that you can express yourself.

If you felt as a child that others in your family were more important than you were, this may be an area you need to explore. Because they're bigger and know a lot more about the world, parents can seem more important to children than anyone, even themselves. If your parents were more focused on their own issues than on paying attention to you, you probably have needs that weren't met. If you grew up under the influence of television and movies, you may have come to believe that you could be special only if you could appear on the screen and be one of the stars. This belief may be particularly strong for you if the people around you spoke of stars with admiration and respect when you were small. But because the business is so overcrowded now, only a tiny portion of actors ever reach star status. The fact is that every individual is the star of his or her own life, and you are special just as you are, whether or not you are successful in your acting career. There are many excellent books on self-esteem and learning to appreciate yourself—the more work you can do in this area, the happier you will be in your life, and the easier it will be for you to get what you want. (See "Recommended Reading," page 171, for some excellent books on self-esteem.)

The idea of success can become an addiction for some people if they're not getting their emotional needs met in other ways; they may even feel there's no point to life if they're not successful. One problem with this belief is that there is really no specific way to define success—some people are very successful in others' eyes, but don't feel that way inside; some people don't have a lot of wealth or power, but are truly happy and at peace with themselves. Success can be hard to define for actors; even if you are incredibly successful in your career, you must still always be looking for the next job. Particularly in the theatre, you can point to credits or roles you have done, and little else; there is no material record of your success. Therefore, it may feel as if any success you've created up to this point can disappear at any time.

Striving obsessively for success can be another version of the "perfection syndrome" discussed earlier: You may keep trying and trying to reach the pinnacle of success without really acknowledging all the small successes you have along the way. Again, learning to focus on what you enjoy about acting and about your life can take off some of the pressure to be a "success" and can help you find ways to create more of that enjoyment in or out of the business. If you're always focused on being successful, you may find, once you've achieved it, that you feel empty.

THE ACTOR'S NIGHTMARE

Many actors have had the dream known as the Actor's Nightmare: You dream that you're in a show but you haven't gotten a script and don't know the lines, so you have to go onstage without knowing what you're doing.

This dream can reflect the normal fears of not knowing how to handle life on a moment-to-moment basis. In the dream, you must play a role you haven't studied, speak words you haven't committed to memory, and move and act in such a way that you help everything to make sense, just as you need to speak and move without a script in life.

If you've had this dream, try going back to the feelings you had in the dream: Did you feel slightly nervous, but pretty sure that you could make a go of it and do a fair job? Or did you feel that you just couldn't function without that script, that you'd make a fool of yourself, and that everything would come tumbling down? The answer to this question may reflect your personal level of comfort or discomfort with the unpredictability of real life.

One of the attractions of acting is that when you're onstage or in front of a camera you know how everything is going to turn out—each moment, each goal and conclusion, is already set up. Even in the midst of very strong emotions, you know where you'll end up. Life is very unpredictable, and it can be frightening to consider that you don't know how things will turn out. But this is also part of the joy and wonder of life: the unexpected, the surprises, the exploration.

It's important to find ways to help yourself feel safe: Visualizing a natural protective energy surrounding you at all times; taking care of yourself in any situations that bring up fearful memories from childhood; reminding yourself from time to time that you're an adult who can deal competently with whatever life serves up. These practices address your "inner child" and, particularly if you grew up in an unpredictable or inflexible family environment, may be crucial exercises for you.

As you begin to reach out and explore life in all its diversity, and as you learn to express yourself more freely with others, be aware of your need to feel safe and respect it deeply. Begin to explore, little by little, the feeling of embracing the unpredictability of life. When you allow room in your life for the new and unexpected, you're also allowing room for growth, for good things to happen in your life.

The pursuit of an acting career, the deepening of talent, and the creation of characters can be one of the most fulfilling pursuits there is. But the more you can bring your feelings and a search for vitality into your life, the more fulfillment you'll find there and in your acting career.

CHAPTER SEVEN

MONEY AND THE ACTOR

Money and all its facets can be a major problem for actors. The most harmful perception is one we grow up with: *Actors Are Poor.* This is a preconception that society plops on our heads from the very beginning. How many times did you hear: "You want to be an actor? You'll never make a living!" On the other hand, perhaps your family has been very supportive: "Do you need money? Are you eating enough? We'll send a check right off"—keeping you believing you need that help to survive.

Of course, it's true that there are large numbers of actors unemployed at any given time, but the danger comes when you buy into this perception without even thinking about it, as if it's a guarantee. If you believe you're going to be poor the rest of your life (or as long as you pursue acting), you probably will be.

Much of the problem stems from the way we were trained to expect that all the good would come in the future—if we work hard now. Parents often hold back rewards in the hope of convincing a child to accomplish or achieve something. But what can happen when we carry this expectation from day to day, week to week, and year to year, is that we are continually expecting to work hard or be poor in the present—and we are always in the present. We never actually do get to tomorrow; by the time we're there, it's today again. So if you're putting your expectation of reward always into the future, you are, in actuality, pushing it away. If you believe that the "pay-off" is on the road somewhere ahead, you may never find it.

You need to find satisfaction in the present, and then work on creating what you want in the future. The more you can believe that your career is happening *now,* instead of at some vague point in the future, the more rewarding the present moment will be and the more you'll clarify for yourself where you are now and where you want to be.

The "Actors Are Poor" stigma can also work in reverse: It can be a good excuse not to concentrate on your finances in a positive way. It may take some honest self-examination to discover whether you use this as an excuse in your life. Sometimes it's hard to pay attention to money matters, to fully accept what you have to pay for the basics of food and shelter (especially living in a major city), and to finally understand that you are the only one who can really take care of yourself. If you find yourself thinking, "I can't deal with this" every time you have to work with your finances in some way (paying bills, budgeting, doing taxes), you may have this pattern of avoidance in your life.

Most people have an unconscious fantasy of being taken care of to some degree, and we are often encouraged by employers, society, the government, and others who want something from us to believe that this wish will come true. Wanting to be taken care of can be a way to avoid truly growing up and taking care of ourselves; we wish that someone else would just take over so that we'd have no more responsibility or risks to deal with. Or it can be a natural side effect of getting in touch with the "inner child" who feels that something is missing—such as support and security—and looks for it in the outside world, as young children must. Do you sometimes wish that someone were taking care of you? Or do you let things slide and let problems mount until someone else has to take care of you? Look at your childhood:

• Did someone always help you out of a difficult situation?

• Do you feel as if you weren't really taken care of on an emotional level when you were young?

• Do you feel as if you gave so much of yourself at some point that it's your turn to have everything given to you now?

These are deep-seated issues which arise from a very vulnerable part of you, so be as gentle with yourself as you can in exploring your feelings.

You are the only person who will always be there to take care of yourself. If you don't, you'll be giving away much of your power to those who do look out for you, or to circumstances that prevent you from providing for yourself. As you connect more deeply with your inner self, remind yourself that as an adult you can take better care of yourself than others did when you were a child.

CAN I MAKE MONEY DOING WHAT I LOVE?

Another obstacle for actors regarding money is feeling uncomfortable being paid for something they love to do. The cause of this discomfort may be an attitude you picked up from your family—namely, that money is something you get only in return for hard work or for something you hate to do. Family attitudes about money can be extremely powerful and deserve as much examination as you can give them. There may have been certain things you had to do to get money, or to get what you wanted, such as doing chores, behaving well, or even being incapable of helping yourself, so that others provided for you. Think back to how you felt about money as a child:

- What did you have to do in order to get money?

- Was there enough money? Or was there always so much that you never thought about it?

- Did your family ever talk about money? Or was money a secretive issue?

- Did your mother or father ever talk about whether or not they liked the work they did for money?

- Did you get the feeling that "money is power" and wish you had lots of it?

The behavior that adults in your family exhibited regarding money and work may also be affecting your present attitudes. Perhaps someone doled out a certain amount to family members, and that amount may have been decided on according to a known or unknown set of rules. You may unconsciously believe that someone else is really in control of money, that you can only have a set amount, or that you have to be a "good kid" in order to get any at all. Over the years, all the things you saw and heard (or didn't see and hear) and the feelings you saw adults express about money and work influenced your current perceptions about them. It's worthwhile to examine these attitudes and the thoughts and feelings surrounding them, because it will help you to make clearer choices in terms of your finances, your life, and the business (see "Recommended Reading" for some excellent books on examining your attitudes about money).

Another pattern that may be holding you back from financial success is the fear that you'll become "commercial" and lose your love for the art if you start making money as an actor. If you're pursuing a career as a professional actor and this seems to be a dilemma for you—all you want to do is act, but you're worried that you'll lose interest if it becomes a real business that starts making you money—you're living in a "double bind," or "damned if you do, damned if you don't" situation. If you've poured all your passion into wanting to be an actor but can't commit to making it a business, you're setting yourself up for unhappiness and frustration because you're bouncing back and forth between two unsatisfying scenarios instead of making a choice one way or the other.

This dilemma may require some careful thought about what you really want, because if you don't gain some insight into the problem, you'll unconsciously find ways to sabotage yourself every time you begin to achieve some success in the business. If you can't resolve the issue, and you still feel concerned that you'll lose your love for the art if you start making money at it, you might want to consider pursuing a career in another area, performing on the side for enjoyment, and leaving the business behind.

Money and Love

One of the most important issues to examine in your life is whether or not on a subconscious level you equate money with love. Attitudes about money in our society have changed to some degree in the last ten years. But many of us grew up watching our parents acquire a more affluent life-style and were bombarded by commercial advertising offering one product after another—always something "new and better"—and those of us who didn't receive the love and respect we needed as children may have thought that money and the things it could buy would make up for what we felt lacking deep inside. This can be a deeply hidden issue and may take a lot of searching inside to discover its existence, because the inundation of cultural messages about money and happiness is so constant.

- When you were upset or had a problem as a child, did others try to compensate by buying you toys or giving you money rather than paying attention to you or helping you?

- Or did someone you'd have liked to spend time with send you money instead of spending time with you?

- Do you find yourself believing ads—that if you buy the right hair product or cologne, it will make a dramatic change in your life?

It's worthwhile to examine your attitudes on this issue, no matter what kind of financial background you come from.

You may also have the feeling that others in your life won't respect or love you unless you make a lot of money. Becoming famous, being a star, with all the power and money that represents, can appear to be a way to get others to love and respect you. Check your family attitudes for perceptions about people who had money:

• Did they seem to command respect in the eyes of your parents?

• Did others in your family seem to want to be close to them?

• Did it seem to you as if people who had money had a better life than you did?

Money can be a very powerful influence and can sometimes cause people to treat those who have hefty amounts of it with an inordinate degree of respect and love. In fact, there are many rich people who are just as unhappy as those without much money, and "making it big" doesn't necessarily include a guarantee of happiness.

Loving others and being loved has nothing to do with how much or how little money you have. It depends more upon a perspective within yourself that you nurture over time, as you begin to share your deepest self with others. Having a loving relationship both with yourself and with others is a part of your life that you need to cultivate to secure the happiness and fulfillment that "making it big" or acquiring a lot of money cannot guarantee.

FEAR OF MONEY

Learning how to handle money can also generate a certain amount of fear, for issues of security and safety are often involved in exploring attitudes about money. Again, your family may have had particular beliefs surrounding money and security: that you could never have enough of it to feel safe; that it's best to save for a "rainy day"; that if you didn't have a steady job, you would end up in the poorhouse. Many people whose parents grew up during the Depression have received fearful messages about money. Fear of not having enough is a particularly relevant issue for actors, because of the nature of the business. You are always looking for the next job and the next paycheck, never sure when or where you'll find them. In today's volatile economy you can never know what *is* enough to feel safe, in any field. True security comes more from self-esteem, more from knowing that you can make it through no matter what happens, than from a large amount of money in the bank.

Some people, conversely, are afraid of making large amounts of money, simply because they're afraid of learning how to handle it wisely. If you haven't often had money in your life, this may be an issue for you. It can also be a way of avoiding having to make choices. This is an area which may require some intensive examination in order to uncover the truth. Be very honest with yourself as you consider these questions:

- Do you feel more comfortable knowing that you don't have to make a lot of decisions concerning money, because there's only enough to pay the bills and eat?

- Do you avoid taking care of things until bills are past due?

- Do you dream of having large amounts of money but have trouble saving even a small amount for something you want?

It can be helpful to start learning more about handling money in small steps, so that you can keep your fears from overwhelming you. Learn to feel safe in dealing with money. Try making a small decision, on any level, about money, based on your own values: Would you like to give $25, or even $5, to a charity you believe in? Would you like to begin saving? You can put away a quarter or a dollar a day, and not even feel it, and you will have made a choice about how you handle your money. Would you like to eat at better restaurants, or spend more (or less) on clothes? Would you like to feel freer about spending money on things you enjoy? Once you have done some exploring in the area of family attitudes about money, find at least one small way to begin making choices for yourself based on your own values, rather than your family's.

SURVIVAL JOBS

It's difficult to concentrate on your art, to be focused and disciplined, when you're constantly worried about paying the rent. It's important to find some kind of work or support that will free you from that fear. Remember, it can take many years to get your career going, and you'll need to be supporting yourself during that period. If you choose a survival job that is demeaning or boring, you'll shortly find that your self-esteem and your mood sinks lower each time you face the daily grind. It's best to find a job that's related to something you enjoy doing, rather than just any job that pays the bills. It doesn't have to be specifically tied to acting; it could be related to another art form or to a field that interested you as a child.

It's important to understand ahead of time that if you are not successful enough with your career to make a living or are not satisfied with the way your career progresses, as the years go by you may begin to identify more and more with the job you chose to support yourself. This is only natural, for you're spending a large amount of time at your "day job," month in and month out, over the years. And if your career doesn't turn out the way you'd hoped, you'll need another way to support yourself. This is why it's important to find a job that's fulfilling to you in ways other than bringing in money. Problems can also arise if you begin to perceive your job only as something you have to do to become an actor. You may find yourself thinking, "If I weren't pursuing a career as an actor, I wouldn't have to do this job," and then resenting acting because it's the reason you have to have the job. If this is a problem for you, there are two ways to think about it. One is that you'd have to be earning a living no matter what, so your acting career isn't necessarily responsible for your having to report to a job. Indeed, you may be willing to work hard in another area just so you have a shot at a successful acting career. The other way to consider it is that perhaps that it's time to rethink your priorities: Is acting that important to you? Or would you be happier doing a more fulfilling job in another field and perhaps enjoying acting on a different level—taking only the acting jobs you want, for example, and not necessarily pursuing it as a career? Sometimes we don't realize that it's time for a change until our level of frustration or anger is very high. This is a good example of how a negative feeling can help you realize that you've grown to the point where it's time to examine whether what you want is what you're getting. Priorities change over the course of a lifetime, and the only way to create the life you want is to examine where you are from time to time and to change your life as your priorities change.

"I'm Really an Actor, But. . ."

Your survival job can also have a profound effect on how you perceive yourself and your life. If the work you do for money is not creative, stimulating, and satisfying in some way for you, you may begin to feel, after a long period of time, that you're wasting your life away with nonproductive work. Often there comes a point in life, usually in the late twenties or early thirties, when one begins to reevaluate life and reexamine priorities. If you've been working at a stultifying job for a year or more, you may begin to feel as if you're "stuck" and there's no way out. In this rocky economic climate, companies may hold onto employees or resist meeting their needs by saying, "Be glad you have a job" whenever you attempt to make your work situation better for yourself. But if the dullness or the stress of your job is driving you crazy, you need to realize that there are always options.

Particularly now, companies often hire temps and consultants in positions that would have been filled by full-time permanent employees five or ten years ago. "Temping" can be an excellent means of exploring a number of different fields and jobs. The point is that while you're working at a survival job and developing your acting career—waiting for it to take off—time can slip by almost unnoticed, and if you don't eventually achieve the measure of success you've hoped for in your career, you can feel like the time has been squandered.

If you feel like you're wasting your life in this way, *now* is the time to do something about it. Don't keep waiting, hoping that something will come along to get you "unstuck"; you can wait years for that to happen and then wake up one day and discover that it never did. Time is your most valuable resource; once it's gone, you can never get it back. You are the only one who can change your life, and the only one who knows what you really want. Explore other options; learn new skills; take a risk. Only you can get yourself out of a rut.

Often people who are involved in the creative arts have a strong need for security in terms of having a steady income. This makes a lot of sense, because the business is so unstable that a steady job acts as a sort of balancer in an artist's life. The problem is that this can cause you to avoid risk-taking in life, simply because pursuing an acting career is a major risk in itself. It's worth it, if you feel stuck in your work life (or in any area of your life, for that matter), to take a few risks: Take a leave of absence from your job and make your living as a temp for a while to find out if other work might suit you better. Or try a new business idea you might have.

The idea is not to be foolhardy when it comes to money, but to learn that you don't have to work at a job you hate in order to make a living. You don't have to continue to feel stuck just so you can pursue your career. Sometimes it's harder to anticipate making a change than it is to actually make the change, but if you keep in mind that a change for the better will help you take better care of yourself, and that your goal is to create a more fulfilling life, it will be easier to take the first few steps.

If you do feel stuck in your work life, look back at your family life and try to perceive the emotional patterns that could explain why you're staying where you are.

• Did you feel you had to work hard at something as a child just to stay in the same place, or just to survive?

• Were you made to feel guilty every time you began to enjoy yourself?

- If you got something you wanted, was there some way that you later had to pay for it?

- Did you often feel there wasn't "enough"—of attention, love, stimulation, free time, money?

Patterns and responses from childhood concerning work aren't necessarily related to chores or a job; they can also be related to feeling that you had to keep up with others, or that you had to put forth an effort for people or do what they required in order to get what you wanted from them. Anything that felt like work to you in childhood may be a part of your response pattern in your present-day job.

Another problem that can arise with a survival job is the feeling of living two separate lives, working as an employee during the day and being an artist the rest of the time. This, too, can be a reflection of childhood, when you knew instinctively who you were within, yet that self wasn't accepted by others in your family, for whatever reasons. Being an actor and having a survival job can be a perfect opportunity to work through this pattern in your current life, following the family "rules" on the job and confining your self-expression to your work as an actor. Again, do some thinking about the past:

- Did you feel as a child that you could express whatever you were feeling?

- Were your ideas and creative solutions to problems accepted and validated by those around you?

- Could you be yourself with some people but not with others?

- Were there feelings, thoughts, and beliefs you weren't able to share and express, that you felt you had to keep in a secret part of your life?

This double-life conflict from the past affects many different kinds of artists, not just actors, and the problem is exacerbated by the view of art that society often takes—that the arts are extraneous and unimportant compared to other aspects of life. Begin to think about this issue now, and try over a period of time to integrate your life more, so that your art and creativity are more closely aligned with the work you do for money.

The workplace also is commonly a repository for family issues. The work you have to do for money may remind you of something you disliked but had to do in your childhood, or your boss may call to mind a parent or teacher. If you're feeling put down by someone at work, remember that you don't have to allow someone to abuse or belittle you. If you come home from your job every day frustrated and angry, you need to do some thinking about what is bothering you, especially on a deeper level, and about how you can make it easier for yourself. If it's comfortable for you, approach those you work with and try to resolve the situation. But if you've tried a number of times to solve the problem and it continues to frustrate you, it may be best to find another job. It's hard to focus on anything, let alone achieve what you want, when your stress and frustration levels are very high. And just as it is in the acting business, there are always more choices, more possibilities—you can always discover options if you take a little time to investigate.

Money is a very powerful issue for most people, on many different levels. Understanding your family attitudes toward money—and your own attitudes toward money as an actor—can help you free yourself from patterns that keep you feeling stuck in certain areas of your life. You can attain more command over your life and the business by working through these issues and resolving them to the best of your ability.

CHAPTER EIGHT

PERSONAL CHOICES: FINDING WHAT WORKS FOR YOU

One of the most difficult aspects of the business is the feeling of powerlessness that it often engenders for actors, who have no control over whether or not they are called back or cast, or even whether or not they are asked to audition. But you can begin to feel more in control of your career by making conscious decisions about areas in which you *do* have a choice. There are a number of areas of the business in which you have a measure of control because you can make more of the choices yourself—about doing your own projects, about whether you will do extra work, about taking classes, and about working in regional theatre, to name just a few. Every actor is different, and what works well for one may not work at all for others; what one actor enjoys, others may not. It's up to you to find out what *your* options are and what *you* want.

Most of us were never taught to trust our own vision and abilities. We were first regulated by the rules of the family, then led through subject after subject in our years of school. There were few choices left to be made. The result of this structured early guidance was that most of us never learned how to choose for ourselves what we wanted or to create a life we could be happy with.

Even in the world of theater, many directors in high schools, colleges, and universities are also on the faculty and, as such, are guiding and teaching the students at the same time they direct them in plays. This can lead students to believe that they'll be guided, supported, and taught in the same way when they work with directors professionally. But in the business this is usually not the case. Also, being guided and led in your schooling during childhood and adolescence can lead you to expect that you'll have guidance in your development of a career. But when this doesn't happen, you may begin to feel powerless in terms of making individual choices about your career. This can lead again to the feeling that someone else has all the power. It may help you to do some thinking about your years of schooling:

- Did you feel you were given the opportunity to make some choices?

- Was it acceptable to make mistakes occasionally, or to give the wrong answer?

- Were you constantly guided and led and only taught to do what the teachers set out for you?

If you didn't get a chance to find your own way and make choices in your education, you may still be following that path, waiting for others in the business to make your decisions for you or tell you what to do.

One way to learn to make your own choices in the business is to be more selective about the auditions you go to. If you go to every audition you possibly can, you may end up feeling you're at the mercy of those who do the casting, unable to choose what you would like to do. You're also setting yourself up to feel desperate to get anything you can, which will show in your relationships with others in the business. Once you begin to be more discriminating and attend auditions only for projects you'd really like to do, you'll start to feel that you're more in command of your career, rather than waiting for someone else to decide which show you'll be in next.

It can seem difficult to take the first few steps toward making your own decisions, taking the reins of your life and career into your own hands, but the more you exercise your own power of choice, the more you'll discover what you like and dislike and what action you can take in order to get more of what you want.

The discussion that follows suggests some areas in which you can exercise your free will, along with some of the pitfalls that you should look out for.

DOING YOUR OWN PROJECT

The one-person show seems to be just the thing these days for creating a successful acting career, and there are several aspects of doing a project for yourself that are attractive: You have the artistic control; you can write material (or have material written) that is perfect for your particular talents; and you don't have to share the spotlight with others—you can be the star. But it can be difficult putting your own project together because of the feeling that everything is in your own hands: You make the choices; you take on the responsibility; and you have to keep it moving forward. There is no one besides you in a position of authority organizing things, giving you motivation, or telling you what to do next. Whether it's a one-person show or a project you've created with a group, you are in charge of the process and the results, and you have to be able to trust yourself at a high level.

You may experience anxiety at first about trusting your own vision and ability to put it all together. After all, the acting business is, by its nature, a search for work—convincing others to see your talents on display and to give you the job, or to keep you in mind for one in the future—rather than a process of creating work for yourself. And because this is what you're used to, you may experience a sense of powerlessness and have trouble making choices and moving forward. You may have particular difficulty learning to trust your choices and sensing what's right for you. The best course to take is simply to jump in and get started. Things will become clearer once you have taken the first step or two, and your innate intelligence will guide you as you go.

If the idea of doing a project or show on your own is particularly frightening or anxiety-provoking, you may be responding to messages you received in childhood:

- Did members of your family create new possibilities and projects for themselves and/or others?

- Or did everyone pretty much follow the same routine, repeating actions or behaviors they were familiar with and waiting for others to show initiative?

- Did you get opportunities to come up with new options for yourself when you were a child, or was that frowned upon?

You may find it easier to make small choices at first: Get together with a friend to work on a scene before you attempt an entire show, or practice by making choices about the auditions you will go to. Remind yourself that you have training and experience which have provided you with a body of knowledge you can rely on. Your instincts in most instances will lead you in the right direction.

Producing a showcase with a number of other actors, instead of a solo act, can also be a rewarding experience. Not only do you share the decision-making power, but if everyone involved supports each other and works toward putting on the best show possible, it can be a most fulfilling theatrical experience. If you are thinking about putting a show together with other actors, ask yourself whom you would most like to work with and work with them. It's much easier to have a mutually supportive relationship with people you can communicate clearly with, and the more carefully you choose the people you work with, the more enjoyable your experience is likely to be.

TO BE OR NOT TO BE AN EXTRA

There is always a need for extra performers in television and film, and some actors are able to earn a living solely from extra work. Some actors even enjoy it; it's a great opportunity to learn how the system works, to meet others in the business, and to watch good actors at work. Occasionally, it may even be a stepping stone to working at a higher level.

Even if the extra work is steady, there is a danger in consistently doing it in lieu of other acting work. An actor can unconsciously begin to think of him- or herself as "extra"—as a part of the set dressing, held at a certain distance from the true life of the film or show, or "not really necessary." If you're doing a lot of extra work instead of playing larger roles, you may lose touch with the unique aspects of yourself that gave birth to your desire to be an artist. You're not getting the opportunity to exercise your talent or to practice your art as an individual member of a theatrical or film ensemble.

If you do choose to perform as an extra, it's important to maintain a sense of yourself as both an important individual and an actor who can create roles as well. If the idea of doing extra work, or if the feelings you have when you do it, are familiar and comfortable to you, it may be a reflection of your past:

• Did you get the message that you should be "seen and not heard" when you were a child?

- Did you feel as if you were unwanted or unnecessary, as if you weren't really a part of the action?

- Did you feel as if someone else (or everyone else) in your family was more important than you?

If the answer to any of these is *yes*, the issue of self-esteem may be an important one for you to work on. Everyone, including you, is an important individual with something valuable to say. Work on finding that part of you that wants to communicate and that needs to be heard.

Although people in the business may say that just because you've frequently been an extra, that doesn't mean they won't hire you for a role, there is still a danger in doing so much extra work that you begin to feel more like part of the crowd than a unique and talented individual. The qualities of conformity and "everyday-ness" may become stronger in you over time, overshadowing your individuality. Extra work, particularly on soaps, can be an excellent beginning step toward more work in the field, toward movement to a higher level. But it can also be a trap that holds you back from expressing your talent to its fullest potential. Don't let yourself feel that you have to do it if you don't enjoy it, just because it's an acting job. And don't continue it if you're only doing it because it's easier than trying to get roles. Many times it seems easier to go ahead and do whatever is in front of you rather than working to get something you want more, but it's usually less fulfilling. Your uniqueness is what's most important. Develop that as much as you can.

TRAINING: HOW MUCH IS TOO MUCH?
Classes can be lifesavers, in terms of being able to work on your craft and polish your skills when jobs are few and far between. Having a solid technique that you can rely on through the years is invaluable, particularly because, with so many actors to choose from, casting people look for a high level of skill and talent. If you do become successful as an actor, you must have a technique that works well for you, helping you sustain your success over the years. Classes are also helpful in terms of being able to network with other actors and of building mutually supportive relationships, and this support can be welcome in a business that is difficult to break into.

Obviously, there is a difference between taking classes and working in the business. Since you are being guided and led by the teacher in a class, it's easy to feel that you can move forward only as long as you have someone's help. If you're not paying attention, you may come to rely on class-work as the primary means to practice your art. Then when you do get a professional job, you may end up wanting the same kind of guidance and support from the director and/or the other members of the cast that you'd gotten in class—and it may not be there. Check your past:

- Did others usually encourage you to seek their help before you did anything on your own?

- Did you seem to need their permission to display your unique abilities?

- Did they give you the feeling that it wasn't safe to step out into the world on your own?

Support is necessary for everyone, throughout life, but if you are relying on others to give you permission to express yourself, to practice your art, or to tell you what to do, you're giving up a lot of your personal power.

If you find yourself following someone else's advice without thinking, stop for a moment and ask yourself if it feels like the right thing for you to do. With all the direction (and sometimes coercing) that children receive, their own ability to discern what is best for them can become rusty or covered over with rules. If you seem to have this problem, make a practice of stopping for a moment to think for yourself before you go ahead and take action.

Ideally, after a certain point, your technique as an actor will become "invisible"—as familiar to you as riding a bike or driving a car. You'll be able to concentrate on bringing your character to life rather than thinking about your technique, just as a guitarist focuses on the art of making music, rather than on finger placement. Technique is itself a personal choice; as you train over the years, you'll find that some of the things you have learned work for you, and some do not. It's up to you to use the ideas and approaches that spark your talent and to discard the rest.

In most fields, once a person gets to the point where he or she is working professionally, taking courses every few years is enough to refresh certain skills or to learn about new developments. And even though musicians practice scales every day, it's usually only as a preparation for actually making the music. After a while, your technique should be so much a part of you that, with a good warm-up, you're ready to work. If you have been taking classes for many years after your initial training, but haven't gotten much work in the business, you may need to take a fresh look at your perspective. Does working in classes feel safer to you than looking for work?

Have you been taking classes for many years because you don't quite feel ready to work professionally? Some actors need much more time than others to assimilate technique and become comfortable expressing themselves within a character, and you must take as much time to train as you feel you need. But if you are feeling stuck in a merry-go-round of constant classes and little or no professional work, you may be holding on to training as a way to avoid the risk of really going after a career.

If you think this might be true in your case, stop taking classes for a short period (a few months or more), and see how you feel. It may free you to spend more time and energy pursuing your career. On the other hand, you may feel you've lost a necessary support. If so, you might try to find other ways to get support for yourself and see if you can devote more of your time and energy to building your career. Only you can know whether or not you feel ready to pursue the business.

On the other hand, some teachers may structure their criticism of your classwork in such a way that they keep you dependent on them. Some may even object if you choose to leave their classes or find another teacher. Be wary if a teacher insists that you remain in his or her class, or says that his or her technique is the only one for you. Actors often benefit from an eclectic perspective on acting technique, and taking classes with different teachers can give you a more well-rounded approach to your craft.

There is a difference between a teacher who might sit down with a student in private and gently suggest that the student could be better off pursuing a different career, and a teacher who calls a student a bad actor or otherwise humiliates the student in front of his or her peers. If a teacher is belittling or harassing you in any way, it may be that he or she is using actors to vent emotions or to feel more powerful. This is another form of abuse, and if you're having this exerience you do not have to put up with it. You need to decide for yourself whether you feel your teacher is helping you grow in your craft or is creating a difficult situation in which to work.

UNIONS: WHAT DOES JOINING REALLY MEAN?

Many nonunion performers believe that becoming a union member will raise them to professional status within the business. But this is not necessarily true. Being a professional, and being treated like one, is based on skill and experience, not simply on a union card. Many actors seek membership years before they are actually proficient enough to do union work. If you get into a union before you have a strong technique and some solid experience to back you up, you may have a difficult time getting work, because you'll be competing with people who have many more years of experience and many more contacts. And once you do get into a union, you will lose the opportunity to work as a nonunion actor, which may mean you won't have as much opportunity to work, take risks, and stretch your talent—to find out what you can do.

If you're a nonunion actor and feel a great urge to join a union, ask yourself if it has anything to do with a need to achieve. It can be hard, when you're going from one show to the next, to feel that you're moving forward, and you may believe that joining a union will immediately move you up a few steps on the ladder. The need to achieve can be another version of the need for perfection. Consider the following:

• Did you feel pushed as a child to accomplish things that could be measured only by an outward show of achievement?

• Or did *you* have to push in order to get what you wanted?

• Did you feel as if nothing much happened in your life?

• Was it necessary to work hard at something in order to feel that your life was worthwhile?

Society today is very achievement-oriented, goading us into believing that if we're not moving farther and faster than ever before, we're falling behind. Everyone moves at a different pace, and if you fall into this "achievement trap," you may push yourself faster than you're really ready to go, damaging your self-esteem and possibly your talent in the process.

Whatever level you've attained, take time to appreciate that you are growing with every experience you have. Whether or not you're a union member, you are still working to develop your craft and pursuing the art you love. Give yourself the space to grow at a pace that's right for you, and when the time comes to join a union, the opportunity will present itself as a natural step in building your career, rather than as a goal you feel you have to push yourself toward.

WORKING IN THE REGIONS

In many cities beyond New York and Los Angeles, an actor's career can build almost naturally because the theater community is smaller. You can go to a few auditions, get in a show, and practically go from job to job simply by word of mouth (assuming you have skill and talent), meeting many others in the community within a short period of time. Many of the jobs may not pay a lot, but if you are more interested in getting the chance to work frequently than in being a star, one of these cities may be for you. Seattle, Chicago, Minneapolis, and other major cities all have fair-to-excellent theater communities, and although some of their larger theaters may cast roles in New York or Los Angeles, many of the mid-size or smaller theaters produce excellent work.

In major cities, you may go for years without getting a role, and one job doesn't necessarily lead to the next. Being an actor there can be much more difficult because the business aspect takes precedence over the artistic. The possibility of success is more often based on luck, on being in the right place at the right time, and on whether your physical look is exactly what they want, than it is based on your talents or on who you are. In the smaller cities, your skills, talent, and personality are what count. In other words, the gambling stakes in New York and Los Angeles are much higher, and your investment of yourself is much riskier. You can be the best actor in the world and still not make it.

If you feel a very strong urge to pursue a career in a large city (or if you're already there), ask yourself if there might be something in your background that made you feel you had to push for "the big one," rather than choose a smaller, friendlier place in which to practice your craft:

• Did you get attention from your family and others only when you accomplished something major—and not for your small successes?

• Is there anyone in your past whose achievements you feel you must surpass?

• Do you feel you need to prove yourself or your talent to someone else by making it in the big city?

If you love big cities, their hustle and bustle and the tough competition, you're probably in the right place. But if any part of you yearns for a slower pace, less competition, an easier life-style, consider pursuing your art in one of the smaller cities. The rewards of working in a more closely-knit community can be great, and the possibility of moving from one role to the next without much of a waiting period can make all the difference in the world.

If you think you might be happier in one of the smaller cities, investigate a number of places. Ask people who have lived or grown up there what it was like, get some tourist information (it can give you a general feeling of the atmosphere), and visit for a few days if at all possible. If the idea of moving away from the larger cities is at all appealing to you, start looking into it now. Your happiness is what's important—not being a "success," following the crowd, or one-upping someone else. From time to time, make a point of looking at where you are, feeling free to reevaluate and change your circumstances as your feelings suggest. Whatever decision you make, in any area, remember that you can always change your mind. You can always return to where you were before, if you liked it better, or try something else. Re-evaluating a decision can often lead to a positive change in your life.

Making as many personal choices as you can concerning every aspect of your life is a good way to help yourself see that you do have some power of choice in terms of the business. As you get more in touch with your feelings, you'll find it easier to decide what's best for you, and you'll be able to trust yourself more in making decisions to get the most out of your life and your career.

CHAPTER NINE

IF YOU DECIDE TO LEAVE THE BUSINESS

Sometimes the business seems like a giant black hole: It sucks up your money, your time, your energy, and your self-esteem, without giving back much in return. If you've spent a number of years in the business without success, or have burned out on trying to make it work, you may be ready to shout "Enough!" Making the decision to leave the business can be difficult, but it may also be the best decision you've ever made.

If you're not working a lot as an actor, or you've become frustrated with the business, if you have even an inkling that you might want to leave, don't push those feelings away. Again, feelings are always there for a reason, and you need to investigate and explore them as much as you comfortably can. It's much better to decide after five, ten, or twenty years that you've had enough and are ready to move on, than to add five, ten, or twenty *more* years of frustration and bitterness.

If you're not comfortable leaving the business right now, but know that if you're not as successful as you'd like to be you don't want to spend the rest of your life pursuing it, you can set a deadline for yourself. Tell yourself that when you're 40 (or whatever age you choose), you will reconsider whether you want to continue, and that you can re-evaluate at any time before that, if you choose. Time can pass so quickly that we lose track of it; setting a deadline to weigh where you are is one way to stay in command of your life.

It's also important to define for yourself exactly what success means to you. For many people, the outward show of money, status, and power defines success, but even people who have these things may not feel themselves to be successful. Being successful can mean something as simple as being happy with your life in general on a day-to-day basis, or feeling that you're moving forward in some positive way, or having the self-esteem and personal power to arrange your life the way you want. Some actors, although they may wish for more, feel successful if they work a few times a year, or even only occasionally in projects that are especially rewarding. Unfortunately, in our society success has usually been perceived in terms of external appearances—not just money, status, and power, but wearing the "right" clothes, living in the "right" neighborhood, or even (by TV commercials' definitions) using the "right" breath mint. But satisfaction and fulfillment—a more basic definition of success—can only be achieved by focusing on who you are inside, discovering your needs and finding ways to fulfill them, letting yourself change and grow, and learning to express the uniqueness that is you in your daily life.

THE NEXT STEP

If you've occasionally thought about leaving the business but are unsure yet whether or not you really want to take the plunge, give it a trial period. Decide on a specific period (a month, two months, or more—whatever you're comfortable with) to stop pursuing the business the way you usually do. Take a break from auditioning, stop buying or looking at theatrical newspapers and books, stop working on monologues—whatever you think will give you the feeling of what it would be like to stop pursuing acting. Even if you think you might want to continue performing without pursuing it all-out as a career, give this a try. At the end of the time period, evaluate your feelings:

• Were you relieved?

• Did it feel like a breath of fresh air?

• Or did you find yourself wishing wholeheartedly that you could just go to that one audition?

If you're yearning to get back to the business, then that's probably where you should be. But if any part of you felt good about taking a break, perhaps you should think more about leaving. You can always change your mind later and go back to the business if you choose.

Because many of your childhood patterns of perceiving and responding can influence your present-day desire to be an actor, it can be difficult to discern whether you really want to be an actor, or whether you've believed that being an actor is the only way to get the attention you want and deserve or the only way to express yourself. In the most basic terms you can think of, answer these questions for yourself:

- What have you most wanted to get from your acting and from your career?

- How do you feel about not having achieved that?

- Can you think of other ways you might be able to get that for yourself?

- What other outlets could you explore that might allow you to express yourself freely?

- How would you like to use the creative energy you've been focusing on your acting?

Thinking about these issues can be difficult and may bring up some painful early memories. But if you can stick with the work, and stand by yourself, getting rid of some of that pain can help you find more joy and satisfaction in your life. Then, whether you decide to leave the business or continue, you will free yourself to live a deeper, richer, more fulfilling life.

MOVING BEYOND YOUR ACTOR IDENTITY

One of the most important issues facing you, if you leave behind something that has been a part of your life for a long time is that, having identified yourself with that activiity or interest, you may feel you're leaving a part of yourself behind. If you have always thought of yourself as an actor and have now decided to leave the business, it's important to find other ways to define yourself. Having used the words "I am an actor" to describe yourself for so long, you may feel your sense of self threatened as you begin to think: "I *used* to be an actor." Human beings equate who they are with the words "I am": "I am a man"; "I am a woman"; "I am 35 years old"; "I am an adult." Being an actor may be the most significant description of yourself you've had for a long time, even for most of your life. It's necessary to realize that you are a person first—that many of the qualities and talents you possess are not directly related to being an actor—and that all the parts of your "actor identity" are still parts of who you are as a person. You must learn to define yourself in new ways, for yourself as well as for others, so that your sense of self is no longer tied only to being an actor.

Something as simple as sitting down for a few moments to explore your likes and dislikes can help you in forming a new identity:

• Are you a person who enjoys museums?

• Do you like to connect with people?

• Do you engage in political debates?

• Do you dislike big parties? Or do you enjoy large groups?

• Are you more action-oriented or more thoughtful and introspective?

The more details of this kind that you can discover about your likes and dislikes, about what you want in your life and what you don't, the stronger the core of your self-knowledge will become and the less you'll need an identity "label" to know who you are.

A particularly crucial area to investigate is whether or not you have looked to acting to supply a fantasy world for yourself. Life can be difficult and painful at times, and acting can be an escape from the realities of life. When children reach the age of two or three, they begin to realize that others will no longer respond to their every need and desire. This can be a rude awakening, and although as adults we hope never to lose the sense of wonder and imagination we had as children, it can be very difficult to mature and take responsibility for the difficult issues in our lives. If you find that your expectations are so high that you're often disappointed, or if you've usually had a hard time waiting until your next role took your mind off the problems in your life for a while, this may be an issue for you.

Try to develop and focus on enjoyable and fulfilling pursuits in other areas of your life to take some of the sheen of fantasy off of acting. Investigate some of the other arts: painting, sculpture, music, writing, dance. Discover for yourself how each relates to the other and how each relates to acting. You don't have to be a Picasso to enjoy painting or a Heifetz to play music—any art can be a very pleasurable pastime whether or not others see or validate your work.

If you discover that there isn't much in your life besides acting that you enjoy, then you need to investigate some new possibilities and build enjoyment into your life in other fields of interest. And remember: With any of this work, if you begin to feel at all depressed or overwhelmed, or if you want help, seek out a therapist or support group or ask a trusted friend to listen to your feelings.

It may also help to realize that there are many ways to use your acting talents other than by being an actor. Acting skills are people skills—not just in terms of working with people, as in the business, but also in terms of having empathy for others, a perception of what makes people tick (used in building a character, for example). These skills can be useful in any number of other professions—sales, psychology, and management, just to name a few. And if you truly love the world of theater and film, there are numerous possibilities for being involved in ways other than acting. You might think about becoming a stage manager, designer, costumer, agent, or director or working in one of the many areas of film production. As an actor, you have gained a lot of knowledge and experience which would be very useful in any of these fields, and you would still be able to express your creativity and use your imagination.

You may feel that if you decide to leave the business after you've spent many years pursuing it then all that time will have been wasted. But since you take from almost every situation something you have learned that you can integrate into the rest of your life, nothing is truly a waste of time— even if you invest years in it and move on to something else. You wouldn't have had those rich experiences if you hadn't been an actor. Still, it may be time to move on and discover the richness in the rest of your life. The skills and ways of thinking that you've acquired as an actor can be wonderful training for other pursuits, if only in the ways you have learned to connect with other people. So take some time to investigate other fields and careers. Something new may spark your interest and start you on the road to a whole new life.

WHAT YOU CAN EXPECT

If you do decide to leave the business, the most important thing to do is find a new outlet for your creative energies, even just a temporary one. Get some paints and start painting, learn to play an instrument, or write in a journal about your feelings (an excellent method for getting more in touch with yourself—see Exercises, page 162). You don't have to look at another outlet as a whole new career; it can be something you do just for pleasure.

But if you try to leave the business without having some other way to express your creativity, it's likely that you'll get frustrated and want to go back to it, even if the business, too, is frustrating. The creative energies you have expressed in your acting need to find another form, and once you have learned to express yourself in a creative way, you will always need that. The mind and the imagination need to release creative energies in day-to-day living.

You may feel like you're floundering for a while. This is natural in any process of change. Even when you feel you're not moving forward, your mind is still in the process of sorting and rethinking, and often the times when you feel that nothing is happening are the times when the most growth is taking place on a deep, inner level. Confusion is a natural part of the process when you're moving forward in your life, and often it means that change for the better is beginning to happen. Children are generally taught that confusion is not a good thing, that the best way to do every-thing is to plan, to be sure of the next step before you take it. But there are times, especially in trying to make your life a happier one, when it's help-ful to surrender to the confusion, so that the best possible outcome has room to present itself. If you have decided to leave the business and sud-denly feel there's a big hole in your life, think of yourself as having an open space in your life that gives new possibilities a chance to present them-selves. You now have a chance to listen to and connect with your deeper feelings and your passion for life.

You'll also need to think about how to get some of your personal needs met in new ways. As you think back to your favorite experiences as an actor, try to discern what it was that gave you satisfaction:

• Did you most enjoy the attention?

• The variety of work situations?

• Working with others on a creative project?

• Learning more about yourself?

• Focusing on your feelings?

All these needs can be met in other ways, once you can define what it is that you want and then look for other opportunities to get it. One of the attrac-tions of acting may have been that it helped you feel special, and this may be an important factor for you, particularly if you didn't get the attention you deserved as a child. It's up to you to find new ways to make yourself feel special: take yourself out for a good meal, spend a day with a favorite book, get a massage, or take a long walk on the beach—whatever makes you feel good. Or ask someone in your life to give you a little extra attention as you go through the transition.

One of the best ways to affirm your specialness is to determine which people you enjoy being with and then to spend time with them. If you spend your time with people you don't enjoy and respect, you're giving yourself the message that you don't deserve respect and enjoyment in your life. But the more you're around people you love and respect, and who love and respect you, the more your self-esteem will grow. Also, you can find and develop friendships with people who are outside of the business, and this will smooth the transition for you.

Don't be afraid of the feelings that come up. As we have seen, the business can be a major repository for childhood feeling patterns, so you may find a lot of repressed emotions "clearing out" as you let go of the business. By all means, if you need someone to listen or to "be there" for you, seek help from a counselor or therapist. Always treat your feelings with great respect and gentleness. And remember that when the deep feelings surface and demand expression, it doesn't mean that you're overly emotional, or not in control—it simply means that you are healing.

Dealing with the Feelings
You may find when you leave the business that you don't feel like doing anything at all, as if there were nothing left that held interest for you. It's quite natural to experience a letdown when you give up something you've been trying hard to achieve. Your body will naturally need a lot of rest and attention; be sure to follow its signals as much as you can. Even if you've lost your passion for acting, and find there's nothing else that stimulates and fulfills you in the same way, there are still many ways to enjoy your life, and usually the passion will eventually return in another form. You must first allow yourself to let go of the past and to rest.

If you're depressed, it probably means that hurt and rejection have built up over time to the point where it just doesn't seem worth it anymore. When you've been hurt or disappointed very deeply, especially over a long period, it can take a lot of time and care to encourage the re-blooming of feelings that you've learned to hide in order to protect yourself from being hurt again. The scenario is not unlike that of a child who has been rejected and criticized so much that he or she must hide his or her heart in self-protection. You may want to take a look at your early feelings in this respect as well to find out whether you may have repeated a childhood pattern of withdrawing from or ignoring your feelings.

It can help to remind yourself that your relationship with acting or the business may have outlived its usefulness for you—you may have learned everything you needed to learn from it, and it may just be time for you to move on to something new. There are times in life when we've grown enough in one way or another that it's better to start out again on a new path, with a fresh outlook, than to keep trying something that doesn't work as well as we want it to work. If you did not achieve the dream you had when you started, it is most likely due to the fact that the business is overwhelmingly difficult and extremely overcrowded, rather than because of any shortcomings on your part. If you feel you've made mistakes in your approach, you need to begin to forgive yourself—this is essential to moving forward and putting the past behind you. Mistakes are a natural part of life and growth, and even a person who makes very few mistakes may still not be successful.

The percentage of actors who pursue professional careers and do not succeed is extremely high. Although it can be difficult to admit failure, it's much healthier to acknowledge that you didn't get what you wanted, and then to move on, than it is to deny the feelings or keep pushing at a wall that won't give. Many children are taught that "if at first you don't succeed, try, try again"; but when you've been expending a lot of energy and getting little in return over a long period, sometimes it's best to give up and turn your attention elsewhere. If you make this choice, it doesn't mean that you're less of a person or that you have less talent than anyone else. Failure is one of the ways we learn about ourselves and the world. It's important to acknowledge the feelings that come up surrounding failure and disappointment, but it doesn't mean a loss of dignity or self-esteem. It may just be time for you to move on and explore other things in life.

As you go through this transition, give yourself as much care as you possibly can and ask for help when you need it. Listen to the voice of your "inner child," and it will help you to heal the hurt. Be willing to spend time alone with yourself, and to support yourself and be gentle with yourself as you let go of feelings you may have been holding back for a long time. Allow yourself to express your disappointment and sadness, and take as much time as you need. Remember that there is a natural ending point for any expression of emotion—you won't feel sad forever. If you can allow your feelings free reign to express themselves for a while, they will wind down of their own accord, and your mood will lift. The more you can clear out some of your feelings related to the business, the better you'll feel, and the easier it will be to forge a new life for yourself that is more satisfying and fulfilling.

CREATING A NEW LIFE

There are many ways you can make the transition easier for yourself. Try the following ideas if they appeal to you, and let them be a catalyst for you to come up with your own plan to help yourself through the transition:

• Spend all the money you used to spend on photos, résumés, stationery, and postage on yourself. Get some of those things you've always wanted but had denied yourself because you felt you should spend the money on your career.

• Or save that money for a period of time and take a trip to a place you've always wanted to investigate, reminding yourself that there are plenty of other ways you can find to enjoy your life.

• Spend all the time you used to spend on auditions and mailings on yourself. Do some of those fun things you always wanted to do, but never had time to pursue. Find a new outlet that allows you to express yourself more freely. Take a short class in one of the other arts so you have a way to release some of your creative energy.

For a number of years, you've devoted your time, energy, and money to pursuing a career in the business, and if you've made the decision to leave, you now have a large number of resources at your disposal that you have previously put toward your career. Use those resources to help yourself find new ways to enjoy yourself, to express yourself. If you were to choose to spend as much time, energy, and money on another pursuit as you have on your acting career, most likely you would achieve great satisfaction and quick growth in that area, simply because most pursuits are not as difficult as that of an acting career.

If you have decided to leave the business, but want to continue your acting in some form, try to find a theater group that focuses on the art of acting, instead of on furthering its members' careers. If you can find a group that operates at least somewhat outside of the business and is intent on furthering the art in the individual and the group rather than on promoting everyone in the business, you can back off from the business aspect of acting and begin again to focus on yourself and your love for the art.

Or join a group that focuses on another interest you have, whatever it may be. You will need to find new ways to connect with others and to get support and attention as you take leave of the acting-is-a-business community.

As you put the business behind you and focus more on yourself and your life, do some thinking about how you might like to change your physical appearance. For a number of years, you've had to conform to your headshot, knowing that if you tried a new haircut, you'd have to get new photos. Now you have the chance to try some new things: Would you like to grow your hair long, or cut it short? Try a new way of dressing—or get more relaxed about your appearance. Transition times can be fun as you experiment with yourself, your looks, your ideas. This is an excellent area in which to let your imagination roam free, as you recreate yourself and your life.

Remember that you are the most important thing in your life—not acting, or "success," or anything else. You are the most important, and you need to learn to treat yourself and your life with the respect and attention you deserve. Take a risk, try something new, begin to experiment with the infinite variety that is life, and move yourself forward into creating a life that you love. It will be well worth your efforts.

INTERVIEWS

This section consists of
interviews with twelve actors
who have spent a number of
years pursuing and gaining insight
into the business. In the following
pages these performers offer their
personal insights into problems
that can come up for an actor on
the way to developing a career.
Some of the actors interviewed, in
opening their hearts and sharing
their deepest thoughts and feeings,
have chosen to remain anonymous.

DEBRA ARMELINO

Debra Armelino grew up in Jersey City, New Jersey. She majored in drama at Catholic University in Washington, D.C. In New York she continued studying acting, voice, and dance.

How did you prepare for an acting career?

After I attended parochial Catholic school, I went to Catholic University, and in my fourth year there I decided to go to London and study. So I did an exchange program for a Liberal Arts degree in London. I wanted a well-rounded liberal arts background and an intensive theater training in a college setting, because I thought it was more important than just going to a specific theater school. Then I came to New York City after college and went to the HB Studio and took some inexpensive classes, found a voice teacher and joined some dance classes.

What made you want to be an actor?

I don't think I chose acting, I think it chose me. I was already the performer in my family. From the time I was a little baby, I entertained everybody, and I seemed to be the glue that held the family together by way of giving them a lot of joy.

I think I took that role seriously. And I was attracted to the spotlight—a ham from the beginning. I was interested in psychology, too, and acting seemed to go hand in hand with that—being different people, pretending to be someone else. I used to watch the old movies on TV over and over and study the actors, and I knew I wanted to do that more than anything. I thought it was a great profession because it combined self-expression with being in front of people and getting attention. I don't know whether I demanded attention as a young child simply because I was a born performer who naturally took that attention, or whether I was a kid just craving attention, and that made me want to be a performer.

How do you feel about marketing yourself as an actor?

That is something I think most artists are unprepared for. I was totally unprepared for that part of it. And that has to do with either chutzpah or self-esteem, which I'm not sure are the same things.

Here you have a world where actors in the business are not necessarily rewarded for their talent, the time they put in, and the education and experience they have. The unfairness of it is very frustrating. When I was young,

I expected to be a star. I certainly was beautiful, and I certainly had a lot of talent. I thought there was no stopping me. And I had a certain amount of success and thought, "This is definitely leading somewhere."

But after a while, I was just going laterally, and it got to be so frustrating that I wanted to take myself out of the rat race of waiting for someone else give me a job. So I decided to do cabaret, where I was the producer, I was the star, I was the writer. I also had to make the flyers, put the stamps on the envelopes, and do everything, so I ended up being a marketing person, even though I hadn't known when I was an actor that I had to be a marketing person. Until that point, modesty had prevailed: I wanted to be seen as an artist, but I didn't want necessarily to have to promote myself. I thought that an agent or manager would take care of that—that's what they're paid for—because that's what the movies tell you.

What has to happen before you can successfully market yourself is self-esteem. They don't teach you that in acting class. I don't think it's just believing in yourself—everybody says, "Believe in yourself!" But you can't really believe in yourself unless you have self-esteem, and you understand that as you get more experience. The selling and the marketing is connected to self-esteem. I had opportunities that I didn't take because I had no self-esteem. I sat in ICM's office with a very top guy when I was about 16 or 17, and he asked me if I knew who Karen Wyman was. I said yes. He said, "Can you sing as well as she can?" I should have said yes, because I did sing as well as she did, but I couldn't say, "Yes, I can," because then I might be considered to be *bragging.*

I think that has to do with self-esteem, with your upbringing, and how you see yourself. Growing up Christian, I was not encouraged to acknowledge my abilities. I'd look in the mirror and see that I was pretty, and people would tell me that I was a good singer, but the other kids would say, "Oh, you're conceited!" I thought I was just being self-aware, and it was confusing. The bottom line is that you have to have self-esteem, which can erode through the years. Even if you start with a solid sense of self-esteem, I think it can get eroded by the hard knocks in the business. But to truly market yourself as an artist requires a very honest self-assessment of your talents and limitations.

How do you feel about agents and casting directors?
Sometimes they don't seem to have the vision that we expect them to have, but I think it may be unfair to expect them to have it. They're in business, so they're looking at you as a product. In that sense, they have a lot to offer

you—if they don't have an axe to grind, if they're not frustrated performers themselves, and if they don't have something they need to prove. I don't think you should take anything personally, because they're looking at you as a product. They're going to make comments on the product. They want to know, bottom line, that there's going to be some money made in working with you. You have to be strong so that you're not hurt by their opinions.

I haven't been around agents and casting directors for a long time. I had to pull back from the business because I couldn't take putting my ego out there to be bashed every day. But that's where self-esteem comes in: If you have it, your ego's not going to be bashed every time. And if it is, you'll pull away enough to come back with renewed strength and vigor, or you'll just quit entirely or find a way to do what you do without depending on others to lay their opinions on you about who you are and what your talent is like.

When I first came into the business, there were people whom I looked at with awe because they had achieved a certain amount of success, and I put them on a pedestal. The problem with that is that you start believing they can help you, that if you could just get to meet one, that person could help you move forward. But then when you do meet one of them, what do you do if he or she happens to be a jerk? Do you go ahead and kiss ass because this is a powerful person, or do you say, "You're a jerk, and I'm not going to bother with you! I'm going elsewhere, and I'm going to make it without you."

That's what it takes—personal integrity and personal strength. In any field that's true, but in show business you can easily be exploited or intimidated by people who are willing to use their power for not such good ends. Maybe they want to take advantage of you or play on your innocence. The important thing to remember is that you can't give up your own integrity, no matter what. If somebody important who could put you in that movie is going to treat you badly or abuse you or take something of yourself away from you, it's not worth the price. Compromising your own values diminishes your soul over a period of time, piece by piece.

Was it helpful for you to back off from the business and get some perspective before going back to it?
Yes, I found it very helpful. I got to a point where I realized that the business was just driving me crazy because I had no control over much of anything. I'd gone through enough hard knocks to ask myself why I was

putting myself through this, and I felt like I had to discover myself. I had never had a break. Even during college I was always competing, and I never felt like I could have a vacation. When you're in New York and in the maelstrom of the business, you feel you have to work all the time. Yet you don't feel like you should take a vacation, because you're not *really* working. I didn't know how to relax in the business and just let it happen. So I decided to take a break and try to find out what investment I had in performing, whether it was that my ego had never been nurtured when I was a child and was clamoring for attention—which is why you can get so crushed from the rejection—or whether it was that I really *loved* the art of acting, the art of performing, the study of it, the nature of it, the development of it, the whole thing. I felt it would be healthy for me to pull away and assess those things and figure out why I needed to do it. I did take a break for a while and tried to live naturally, asking myself, "What would I do if I wasn't doing this? What would I do if I didn't buy *Back Stage* every Thursday?"

So I stopped buying *Back Stage*, and I stopped getting caught up in, "Oh, I'll go to this, and I'll go to that, and this audition is at 8 AM on Thursday, and if I run, I can make it downtown to the Public by 10, and then I can run back up to the Equity lounge by 12:30 for another call, and then I can go to dance class, and then. . . ." I was driving myself crazy, because I've always been achievement-oriented. And I just didn't have enough of a life. Acting wasn't giving me enough that I wanted to sacrifice the rest of my life for it. You do without furniture or the peridontal work you need because you need $800 for headshots and résumés. There were a lot of sacrifices through the years that I chose to make, and I started to get resentful about those sacrifices because there was so little return. It's not worth giving up everything for.

What happened when you stood back and looked at all the rushing around and the sacrifices? What happened when you gave that up for a while?
It felt good, because I felt more in control and not so reliant on others to assess me as a talent. I had always been fishing for someone to tell me I was talented, and when they didn't, it made me insecure. I didn't feel I was worth anything. I had to pull away to get some security within myself. I kept thinking early on in my career that I had to be compulsive about the business in order to get somewhere. People instill that fear in you: "Oh, you can't stop! Oh, you're getting older, and if you want to go to L.A. you'd better go now!" Everybody has opinions.

You can't buy into that hysteria in any way, even though it's hard to resist; it's so easy to believe what everybody says. I realized that, in large part, I was living my whole life in front of an audience, and I needed to stop listening to that audience telling me what to do with my life. So the pulling away was good, because it made me disengage from everybody else's opinions, from their being so vitally important, and from needing everybody else to tell me I was talented and worth something.

Any advice for actors just starting out?
Have your anchors in life—people you can rely on as a support system no matter what, whether that's your family or your best friend. It's very important because of the rejection in the business. Another thing is to not take the rejection personally. It's all just dollars and cents in the business. I used to resent that, because I wasn't into money, but the rest of the world *is* into money. The point is that, in any area of the business, you will have to find an audience to be successful, whether you fill the small lounge at Harrah's casino or star in a Broadway show or a billion-dollar movie, but you can't be so hungry that you're willing to pay them and be exploited.

Look around and see the whole of life, not just the piece of it that is the business. And assess yourself in other ways. You have to know your assets and your liabilities outside of the business too, so that you have a fuller life. You can try the business full-throttle for a while and then later decide to do something else. You need to learn to see yourself clearly, and that happens through the people who really know you, your friends or family, not through other people in the business. Find a theater group that supports you, a place where you can fail and look like a jerk, because that's where you're working out the kinks so that you can be brilliant.

Look at what's selling out there, what kinds of actors are really getting work, and look at how you measure up to what's selling. Think about whether you want to fit into what's selling or to be a completely unique animal and try something different, as Roseanne Barr did. Self-awareness is just so important.

Anything else?
I believe there's a difference between arrogance and self-acceptance. Sometimes self-awareness can look like arrogance. To be an original, you can't always think along with the crowd—you have to look at what you really believe and follow it in spite of everyone else's opinions. You have to be aware of what's hot and what's not in order to market yourself, but you can't measure or judge yourself based on that. Whoever you are, that's what you have to use.

JOHN B.

John B. grew up in a suburban town in Massachusetts. He studied psychology and philosophy at Yale University. John moved to New York to become an actor with no prior training in acting.

What background did you bring to New York and your decision to be an actor?

When I think about my background, it was a fairly stable and normal life— no major traumatic upsets or anything. I consider myself very lucky in that respect. I went to public schools and took a year off between high school and college, I guess to get less nervous about going to college. I had a part-time job as a peer counselor at the high school I graduated from, which amounted to having a form of therapy. That was a major event in my life, and I was very happy that year.

I don't know exactly what I had in mind studying psychology and philosophy at Yale, but I think I was fulfilling a need to have some sort of legitimate background in some field other than theater. I was doing what I was "supposed to do" by going to college, as if I owed my parents something because they were sending me there. I didn't want to terrify them by going into a field they had no understanding of—it was just an alien world—and I didn't want to terrify myself either, because it was alien to me, too. I worked at a factory near my home town for about six months after college, and made a little money, and then I moved to New York to become an actor.

Why an actor?

Being an actor was a childhood dream of mine from as far back as I can remember. I don't really know why. I was in a couple of shows in college, and I worked one summer of summer stock, doing very small roles. I didn't have any kind of technique for being onstage. I had a lot of wrong ideas about how to function as an actor. I was a fairly entertaining person in a spontaneous social setting, which I thought would translate more or less directly onstage. But it just didn't work that way.

When I got to New York, I really didn't know anything about the business. About three months after I moved to New York, I went to an open call for a children's theater company, a combined Equity–non-Equity call where they saw both union and nonunion members throughout the day. They were typing people, and I was one of the people who got picked to audition. After a couple of weeks, they called me in for a callback. I had an unusual idea of how to read the scene, and so I got the part. It was a touring show, a paying job, and I'd gotten it three months after coming to New York, so I thought I was way ahead of the game. Then we started rehearsing, and I got fired, because I just didn't know what I was doing. When I had auditioned for the show, I knew there wasn't a specific way it was supposed to be, so I made up something that was creative, and it worked well. But what I believed actors did, fundamentally, was to wait for the director to tell them what to do, and then try to do exactly that; a good actor was a person who was the best "clay," who could do whatever the director or the script said to do. Now I believe that's absolutely wrong.

At first, when I imagined myself being onstage, I could imagine myself really being great and giving a great performance. But I couldn't actually *do* it—I didn't know how. I thought if I only knew what I was supposed to do, then I would be able to do it, but that's not true—it doesn't work that way. I was extremely limited and didn't really realize it. I had no idea how slowly you improve and grow as an actor.

Every actor has moments when everything works great, and it's all there, but to be able to do that on a more or less consistent basis, and not just hope that "this is one of the times when I'm going to be good," takes a long time. I don't know anyone who is a really good actor who hasn't trained for a number of years.

When I got fired, I knew I wasn't performing well, and it was traumatic. The guy who fired me was shaking with anxiety about having to fire me, but he did intimate that I was probably one of those people who would never be an actor, because I didn't have the basic ability to walk around onstage and seem like a real human being. At that point, someone suggested that I get some acting training, which I thought would be a good idea. But I didn't realize how *much* it would help me.

I was determined not to quit on the basis of that one experience, so I took improv classes, went to the T. Schreiber Studio in New York, and then decided I wanted a more comprehensive program. So I went to the New Actors Workshop, which combined scene study and exercise work with a pure form of improvisation. At the end of my first year in that program, the principal acting teacher recommended that I go into therapy to work on certain personal, emotional barriers that were interfering with my development as an actor. So I've been doing that for five years, and I think it's helping.

I gradually realized over the years of my training that what is written in the play and what the director gives you is only a skeleton: You have to make most of it up yourself. Even if it's a great play, you still have to fill it out from your own imagination. And when you're up there, and you're actually doing the acting, it's *you,* not somebody you're pretending to be. That's what people want to see—they want to see you. I don't think in acting you're supposed to hypnotize yourself into some perfect state of concentration so that you think you are not an actor but are actually the character and that what's happening in the play is what's really happening. There is always a part of you that knows you're acting, that knows what's really happening, even if it's way off to the side. If you're a complex person who behaves differently in different situations, then you will behave differently in one role or play than in another. But it's still *you.*

Do you think you went into the business with the objective of being a working actor, or being a star?
I don't think I made a distinction between being a star and being a working actor. I thought I'd be a working actor, and go to the next thing and the next and the next—not necessarily making the biggest movie or having my name on the cover of *People* magazine, but knowing that the next project would always be there. I think that's what being a star meant to me.

As I imagined it early on, the appeal of being a star, aside from the obvious things like the fantasy of constant, limitless attention, was that you'd never have to worry about working again. Somehow, stardom would be like a big playground that's built for you, and all you have to do is play in it—a sort of professional Eden, where the fruit is just there on the tree and all you have to do is take it when you want. And you don't have to work so hard or not know where the next thing is going to come from, or if it's going to come at all. I know that the reality is not like that. I'm not a star, and I don't know any personally, but I'm sure that, as a star, you have a new set of concerns and a new set of worries, and that you don't stop working and trying to create the best projects for yourself that you can.

But I had believed, and I think a lot of young actors have believed, that just getting there is going to make a dramatic change in your life. There's something childish about it; after all, being an actor is being paid to play. There's the childish wish to be taken care of, the fantasy that all you have to do is what you feel like doing. As long as you follow certain basic rules, you can just go out there and have fun, and everyone's going to take care of you. They're going to give you money and an audience, put your clothes on you, do all the things that parents do for children.

A lot of actors still believe that you can get to a place where you don't have to worry anymore about whether or not you're wanted, but that's not realistic. There's a belief that you'll have an agent who will send you out, you'll do your thing, you'll get hired, and everything will be taken care of. Almost all the actors I know who've expressed a desire to get an agent believe that the agent is going to make a big difference in their careers and their lives. They believe they'll start getting quality auditions and won't have to wait outside and be nobody. They'll be actors with appointments who've been asked to come in and that that's going to be ongoing—that once you've got an agent, it's sort of downhill from there. But nobody I know who actually *has* an agent has had it turn out that way. Agents get excited at first and send you out, and if you don't book something fairly quickly, they don't send you out anymore. So you're back where you were, wishing someone would take care of you. I think the reality is that you have to keep making it happen for yourself. Even if you're Dustin Hoffman, you still have to work very hard to keep working.

So the belief that having an agent will change everything is a reflection of wanting to escape the work of promoting yourself?
Yes. Even if you're a major star, you still have to promote yourself—if nothing else, to the public, to your director, or to the writer. You can't stop putting in the effort, all the time, every minute, to make your movie or play successful. You always have to take care of yourself. And as long as you're living in the belief that at some point you won't have to do that anymore, you're going to end up in a collapse.

I also think that you can't make it your whole life. You have to work at it, and it has to be your job, but not everything you are. Of course you want to care about the auditions you're doing, but making it your whole life is a formula for disaster. Not only does it injure you emotionally, it injures your performance, your acting; it makes you less effective, less appealing as a performer. You are limiting yourself if you think that life is all about the next audition. You're limiting who you are as a person and what you're capable of, and I think it diminishes you. And people can sense that. People want to see someone who has a lot inside, and that's not going to happen if you make acting your whole life.

How did you decide to stop marketing yourself?
Well, several weeks ago I went to an open call for a film that was being conducted by a famous director. I think people later estimated that about 3,000 people showed up. That day we had the biggest snowstorm of the year, and

people had been waiting outside in the cold and snow—in period costume, as requested—since the night before. We were sort of herded up to the tables where they were collecting photos, and the director was standing behind his assistants, nodding and smiling occasionally, and they offered us cups of chicken soup. The director didn't even talk to anyone, but he had invited the press, so I think it was a big publicity stunt, and maybe a way for him to get juiced up for the project, to see how many people he could get to come out to be in one of his movies. He didn't seem to feel sorry at all that it had turned out to be such bad weather. He was enjoying what was happening, even though people were really suffering from the cold and wet. I felt there was something sadistic about it, and something masochistic about the actors who were doing it. Although there's a remote possibility that the director would call you in from your photo for a legitimate audition, you're in a very bad position if you're competing against 3,000 other people, no matter how great you are. That's just not the way to go about it. And yet people stayed, and I stayed, believing that this was our best chance, as remote as it might be, to get in the movie, which I would have loved being in.

This goes back to the childishness, the passivity, and the acceptance of someone else's rules: If you just fulfill those requirements, if you do what Daddy says, then you'll get what you want from Daddy, whatever it is you're hoping for. After that audition, I became very depressed, because even though it was a more exaggerated and grotesque version of auditions I'd been to before, it was still exactly the same thing. Usually you get to do a monologue or at least meet the person who's casting, usually the weather isn't that bad, and usually there aren't 3,000 people, but it was the same thing. And for me that's what it took—experiencing that huge a nightmare made me say, "I can't do this anymore." I just felt there was nothing left for me. In the last couple of weeks, I've found out about some possible projects, and I'm feeling better. But that was just devastating.

Now, if I want to do something, I'm only going to do it if it can be a good thing for me. If I'm only doing it so that an agent, a producer, or writer will see it, I'm not going to do it. Because, although there is a possibility that one of those things could happen, I know from experience that it's very remote. It has to be worth doing whether that happens or not. Even if I do invite agents and producers to come see it, that's not my primary objective. And that's a big change for me. I don't know if I've ever approached anything in that way. You do it because you want to do it, because it's worth it in itself, not because it could get you something. You have to find your own way, make your own road, by doing what it is that you love, by using what's unique about you.

ROBERT BOWEN, JR.

Robert Bowen, Jr., grew up in a small town, Durham, Connecticut. He attended the Rhode Island School of Design and trained to be a designer. He began his act-ing career after moving to New York City in 1972.

Did you always want to be a performer?

I graduated from a Catholic boys' high school, where they used to have us fill out questionnaires about what we wanted to do in the future, and I would always put down "performer" or "art teacher." "Art teacher" was just to satisfy the academic atmosphere I was in. I really wanted to be a per-former. I went to art school instead, and afterward I came to New York and started taking dance and acting classes. I had originally wanted to be a dancer, but I got hooked on acting.

How do you feel about marketing yourself as an actor?

I think it's dismal. I don't think the artist sees it as a creative function. I once heard someone say, "When money comes into the picture, artists feel their humanity is jeopardized." I think that's true, because to me, creating is like flying, and business is more like walking. You lose the sense of spon-taneity in the business that you have in the art. As artists, our art is an extension of ourselves, and yet business is really not—it just doesn't seem to come naturally. Art is process-oriented, but business is product-oriented. However, the artist can function creatively within business. For example, I used to do a lot of creative things with postcards and letters to people, and it did net me some response. But it wasn't the sending of the card or the mailing of the résumé so much as it was that I put my personal stamp on it. I found the only way I could do that was by doing it with the confidence that, whether or not it was rejected or responded to, it was still a legitimate part of me and I had to take the risk in showing that to people. If you pay attention to what you're doing, to the creativity you put into it, and to what you learn from it, rather than whether or not you get a response, it gets eas-ier. Being personal and immediate, extending yourself and being willing to make a connection, willing to be honest—I think those are chances we have to take.

I hate the word "networking," but the dynamic is that if you're not out there meeting people and connecting with them, you're not going to get anywhere. So now I pick out a few people I want to keep in touch with. I don't try to keep in touch with everyone or do mass mailings anymore; I just pick people who have shown interest or with whom I would like to work, and I do my best to keep in touch with them on some kind of consistent level.

You've been in a number of shows in the last few months. How do you feel about going through the rehearsal period? What's your response to directors?

I had been out of the business for a while, and what I've found after being away from it is that now I go into a project with a sense of frustration and the feeling that I have to hurry up. I feel I have to make up for lost time, to enter into every new project being omniscient—knowing everything and having all the answers—so that I'm not a drag on the rehearsal process; I'm not proving my inadequacy, stupidity, or naïveté by asking questions. I sometimes feel threatened by all the communication, the "dialoguing" one needs to do in a collaborative art, because I feel it's going to make them think I'm not as experienced or as good or as smart as they thought. I feel like I have to prove myself.

In acting, you can't see what you're doing, so there's never really any tangible product or outcome you can look at and say, "I did it right." There are times you feel terrible about a performance, and yet people are moved; other times, you feel you were absolutely glowing, that this was a remarkable moment in the history of theater, but people are unimpressed.

It's important to strike a balance and know that as long as the story is told, we've done what we're really there to do. We're not there to be fabulous actors, we're there to get the story across. I can do my job very well, as long as I'm not worried about how well I'm doing it.

Right now I'm terrified of the actor–director relationship, and I think it's because in the last couple of shows I did not have an essential rapport with the director. It was a flawed relationship partly because of my own insecurities, but also because these insecurities were magnified by my lack of faith in the director. And so I kept turning those guns on myself, thinking it was all my fault.

Now I'm working with a young director who works in a way I think is good for me. Basically, what he creates, above all, is an environment in which it's safe to expose oneself—not just as an actor developing a character, but as a person with ideas and philosophies and misgivings and insecurities. There's room for all that to be expressed, especially among the actors themselves. And that's important for me. In the last show I was in, I felt I was working with a roomful of people just building characters, and even though we were together, we never had a real exchange of any kind. We were constantly watching ourselves and each other relative only to the work being done. So I felt frightened of failure, because the only thing they knew of me was my work; they didn't know who I really was, and vice versa. It's important to me that I feel connected to the people I'm working with, on a human level—that there's a sense of community which isn't just based on having a task in common, but which includes who we are as people and the permission to discover that as we go along.

The professional theater is scary in that respect: The conventional audition and rehearsal process doesn't allow a lot of room for building a safe environment, which people need when they are revealing themselves. You have to build a sense of trust.

Why did you choose to take time off from acting?

I'd gone to the Royal Academy of Dramatic Arts for their summer program in 1983, and while I was there I went to a lot of theater. And it finally dawned on me that these actors did this as a craft, that acting is a craft. Like plumbers or any other craftspeople, some are true artists at what they do, and some are not. I knew there were a lot of things I could do well as a craft, from which I could get just as much satisfaction as acting. I didn't really make a decision about it, but when I came back to the United States my heart just quit and the ambition was gone. The recognition of my talent was there, because I'd gotten very favorable responses in London, but I just didn't want to audition any more. It was very clear for me.

I felt I had rejoined the human race, because I was one of those blessed people who was able to let go of a burning ambition, an obsession. My fundamental realization was that we create theater, it doesn't create us. I don't get my identity from theater. For many years, I thought acting was what I *was*, not something I *did*, and if it was something that I was but I wasn't doing it, then I didn't exist. If it had been something I *did*, so that there was a sense of "I" that existed prior to the activity, I would have been merely frustrated, not nonexistent, if I wasn't doing it. I needed to go through a period of living real life, being a person on the planet who lived and breathed and had things to say or didn't—not constantly on a search for a job in the theater so that I could be validated. I needed to be validated in my day-to-day life. And that was really nice, because my whole life was suddenly focused on myself, rather than on what I was going to audition for, who was casting what, and whether I'd missed out on some opportunity or felt jealous of people who got work.

My feelings don't consume me anymore. I let them happen, and they burn out, but they don't define who I am. I've learned to take things less personally. That's difficult in an art, in performing especially, because actors use their own humanity as the backdrop. I knew when I left the business that I could always go back, that no matter how old I was the theater would still be there and there would be some role I could play. I finally realized that my having talent didn't mean that I had to do something with it. So I became bigger than my talent, rather than letting my talent define me as a person.

Do you find there's much of a difference in how you approach the business and the art this time from when you were in it before?

I understand it much better now. I understand the need for remaining in contact, for garnering and nurturing contacts. I don't feel that I'm hypocritical—that I have an ulterior motive—as I did years ago, because I am now seeing agents, casting directors, and directors as craftspeople in their own right. Without actors, they can't do their jobs either. I can see now that they want to work with people they like, trust, and respect, just as I do. I don't want to audition for some jerk, just because he or she is a casting person. And I don't want to pay people 10 percent if they're of dubious or questionable repute. And if *I'm* making those kinds of choices, so are *they*.

There is room for personal exchange, for human contact. You can pick and choose whom you want to work with, based on their sense of your worth as a human being, not just on what they can do for you. I'm not as afraid of being personal anymore. A lot of actors probably shy away from business work because it seems so impersonal. I think we whitewash ourselves—writing a really generic cover letter, for instance, rather than really saying anything, because we're afraid of saying the *wrong* thing. What most actors fail to realize is that they have the prerogative to say no. We're so busy being worried about people saying no to us that we feel we have to say yes all the time. So we lose our own sense of power in the exchange.

Any advice for actors who are just starting out in the business?

Just keep going. And make sure that what you weave into your work while you're developing your skills and your business acumen is an awareness of yourself that's spiritual, so that you're blanketed with a sense of being unconditionally loved. Your worth isn't based solely on your ability to do good work. The ability to do good work actually comes from a sense of well-being. We can't work well when we're panic-stricken or full of fear.

There's the whole idea that the crazier people are, the better they are as actors: Some people who are incredibly good actors are not necessarily stable people, but being crazy isn't a prerequisite for good acting. I know some people who are very stable and absolutely brilliant actors. Acting is an art, a form of self-expression, and people shouldn't just do it because they're crazy or needed attention as a child and didn't get it. Those reasons certainly can be motivators on some level, but fundamentally an actor is a person who loves to investigate and portray humanity, who is in love with human behavior. I think that anything else is just showing off.

I learn so much through acting. Acting's not just what I have to say, it's what I learn. It broadens my compassion for humankind, my ability to understand why someone might do or say certain things. It forces me to get out of my own comfort zone. It includes being very uncomfortable and very unsure, but that is no indication, ultimately, that I'm doing it incorrectly.

I left the business because I needed a major adjustment in my life perspective, and that included getting out of acting. Then, to start again in midlife was major, because I realized I didn't have the time I had before. I only have the time I have now ahead of me.

As an actor, you can only bring what you are to the art. So the older you are, and the more life experience you have, the more you have to offer in terms of the art.

MARGARET BURNHAM

Margaret Burnham grew up in a small city in Ohio. After attending a liberal arts college, she trained at the National Shakespeare Conservatory. With her home base in New York, she has worked in regional theater, summer stock, independent films, and showcases.

What was your route to becoming an actor?
When I was in high school, we had a very small theater program and pretty much did shoestring productions. In college, I didn't decide right away what I wanted to major in. The college was very limited—there was only a speech department, with a "theater concentration." I was encouraged by a couple of people to pursue theater in some form, and I thought I might want to be a director or stage manager. But there was no provision for students to do that, until you got to be a senior; then you could do an independent study program as a director. I wanted to do a one-person show, but

I was encouraged away from that and encouraged instead to do research, because I excelled at it.

The summer between my junior and senior years, I had an internship at the Great Lakes Shakespeare Festival, which is a major regional theater, and by then I had begun to prove myself a bit more as a performer. But I had no chance to change my opportunities at that point because everything was set up for the rest of my academic career, geared to the research.

I had auditioned for the National Shakespeare Conservatory and was accepted, so I moved to New York right out of college as a very, very green 22-year-old. After I finished the Conservatory, I immediately did summer stock. I've now been in the business about 15 years altogether.

How do you feel about marketing yourself as an actor?
I think it's the hardest thing in the world, I really do. For the most part, creative people don't have a natural bent toward business and marketing. Also, a woman of my age was trained to be modest, and that makes it harder. I also seemed to be a particularly naive person who never really realized, in the beginning, what the business entailed. I hadn't been exposed to any kind of business experience. I never really did pursue the soaps very much, or commercials. I was never very good at the business aspect of acting. I think that's the great downfall for many people.

The first time I had professional pictures done, I did one mass mailing to agents and got three calls. But I was so uninformed—I just had no clue that you really had to hound them. I didn't follow up or send postcards. I guess I thought they would come after me, once they knew I was there. I didn't understand the numbers that were against me, which I don't think were even as bad ten or fifteen years ago as they are now. Also, there were many more job possibilities when I was in my twenties than there are now, and that has changed my perspective.

Recently, I hired a business coach. Working one on one, she's helping me learn how to make phone calls—which is the hardest thing for me—and finding other ways to look for work. She helps me set goals so that I have something very specific to work toward. There are ways you can target the market so that you're looking in a specific area rather than for just any job, and that makes it easier. There are so many options out there, you just can't do them all.

I finally have pictures I'm really happy with, and that makes it easier to send them to people. Partly because I'm naturally modest, and partly because I have a confidence problem, it's hard for me to say right out: "I can do this, and I'm the person for you." If I can show them I can do it, that's a little easier. Even then, that's where all the demons come in and make you question and doubt yourself, which makes you seem less confident, as if maybe you can't do the job. And then they won't hire you. My business coach is also helping me tote up all my accomplishments, so that I can see what I've done, instead of just looking at what I haven't done. And that helps to keep me going.

How did you finally get the photos you feel good about?

This is the fourth or fifth time I've gotten professional photos done. Each time they've gotten better in one way or another, partly because I've learned what to ask the photographer, and partly because I've been more willing to spend money on myself. It is a business investment, a huge cash outlay, and you have to be willing to say what works for you, and what doesn't, to get photos you're really happy with. Because if you look great, and your monologues are good, but your photos don't support that, then you move down a notch. They'll think you're not ready to book, not ready to be hired, not a complete package.

What I did differently this time is that I gave myself plenty of time. I didn't have to have the photos for a particular audition, so I had time to choose the pictures. And with the feeling that I don't have to rush comes an increased sense of self-respect or self-worth. The way I'm approaching a lot of things now is that I'm trying to make it much more on my own terms, trying to fulfill my own expectations rather than other people's. It's a cliché, but I'm trying to represent myself as the best me I can be, as opposed to trying to do what other people want or expect. It makes me feel a lot more comfortable and a lot less anxious, and I can't help but think that if I'm being more true to myself, it will show through in my work and in the marketing.

How do you feel about agents and casting directors?

I've had little experience with agents. They are really frightening to me, because I feel like they're sitting in judgment on me. That may be my own lack of confidence, but in some ways they do hold power. They submit your picture and résumé to someone else, the casting person, who holds another kind of power. One of the few times in my career that I had an agent sending me out, he couldn't get me an appointment. He submitted me all the time, but could never get the casting directors to give me an appointment.

Part of the reason I find it frightening is that they have that power. Casting directors seem to me like another wedge between the actor and the job; they're yet another person who has to pass approval to some degree. They do contribute to the overall product, but they're still kind of a middleman, as far as I'm concerned. The agent sends the photo to the casting director, instead of to the director or producer, who is usually more involved with the project. But the casting director and the director or producer might have different ideas, so the director or producer might not end up seeing people who are really right for the role, because the casting person doesn't bring them in.

Have you ever thought about leaving the business?

Absolutely—every two or three days! I don't know what keeps me going. Except that when you're doing a show, you're getting that positive response. There is something about the energy that you get addicted to—having those heightened emotions, and having to put yourself on the line to do it in front of people. That's one of the things that keeps me coming back: It's very energizing. I feel more awake. Sometimes, not doing it, or staying at home, or even working in an office under somebody else's direction, is "easier," because you don't have to make choices. But that's also a kind of depressant; it puts you to sleep.

I never have officially quit the business, as some of my friends have. The few times I've backed off from it I have needed to pull my life back together, or needed money, or one thing or another. Two months before I got married, I was offered a national tour of *Romeo and Juliet* playing Juliet, which was a major opportunity for me. But I had already had the wedding invitations printed, and everything was ready to go. So I had to make the choice: "Is it life, or is it a four-month tour?" And that time I chose life. I wasn't unhappy with the decision.

There have also been dry periods and other times when I've been so busy that I couldn't concentrate on the business. But every time I seriously think about quitting, the first thought I have is, "What would I do? What else would make me happy?" And I've never discovered anything that gives me that same kind of "high." Some people get it from downhill skiing, or skydiving, or long distance running. But I have never found anything that duplicates the vitality of doing shows, so that I don't feel like I'm swathed in layers of gauze or only half living. I think I still have to keep doing shows, so I can wake myself up periodically. So that's what's kept me in it: I've never found anything else that makes my juices flow.

I have found other things that I like, but not in the same way, or to the same degree. When I start looking for another profession, it seems like so much effort. If I want to be a physical therapist, I have to go back to school; if I want to strike out into the business world, I have to start at entry level, below $20,000 a year. These things will take so much effort, or will be such compromises for me, that unless I'm absolutely sure about it, I'm not going to do it. It's also the path of least resistance for me, because a lot of the people I know are in the business. And somehow, always when I'm at the depths, somebody has asked me to do something, or something has come through to buoy me back up, to remind me what it is that I like about it.

What advice would you give actors just starting out in the business?

I don't know how you can acquire business sense without experience. There's just so much to learn about how the business works. Anything you can do to *not* take it personally is important. Just to say that is not enough; you must somehow realize how business decisions are made, and that it really doesn't have much to do with the individual person. I didn't have a particular area of the business I was especially good at. I was pretty good at a lot of things, so I spent too much time spreading myself thin, trying to focus on too many areas. I have a broad range, there are a lot of things I can do, and it's hard for casting directors and agents to admit that; it's easier for them if they know exactly where to put you—commercials, or musicals, or whatever.

And theater is changing, because of finances. Everything is so expensive to produce now that fewer shows get on, so the top stars become people who are fighting for supporting roles, and they push the supporting actors down to the smaller roles, pushing the people who are trying to get the small parts off the bottom of the ladder. I think I'm a bit resigned to the idea that I might not ever "make it," and I'm kind of okay with that—it doesn't really bug me now. Five years ago, I probably wouldn't have been able to say that without breaking into tears. But now I know I will still be a person, have a home to live in, and be able to make money to eat food. I have a good life. And I think I'm a stronger person than I was, partly because of the struggle and trauma.

So your life is more important than whether you make it or not?

Yes, it is. Whether I make it or not is so ephemeral and so out of my control. When I was first starting out, I read the statistics, I knew that it was hard, but I don't think you can accept that when you're starting out. I think you still have to have hope. There's no one way to make it, there's no formula, and it's different for everybody. It's such a chancy thing, and the way is littered with people who don't make it, or who make it to a degree different from what they expected. It's not like most other fields, where you get training, work your way up the ladder, get settled into a good job, and stay there or move on to something better. There aren't certain steps you can take. It's not linear at all—it's a meandering path, and very uncertain.

Right now I'm trying to find a balance. I'm very, very lucky, because I'm happy in my personal life, and that is making a huge change in how I approach the business. When I was a lot younger, if I didn't have a relationship or a home that I liked and I wasn't making money and getting theater work, there wasn't anyplace I could *retreat* to—all those fronts were bad and scary. So when I went to an audition, I needed something to buoy me up, and if I didn't get a callback, it seemed to reflect how bad my whole life was. Now I have a nice home and a husband that I love, and I know I can make money when I need to. So if I don't get that next theater job, it doesn't bother me nearly so much. I still enjoy it, but I don't need it so much.

ANITA KEAL

Anita Keal grew up in Philadelphia and studied acting at Syracuse University. She lives and works in New York City.

How did you decide to become an actress?

I don't think I can ever remember not knowing that I would be a performer or an actress. My memories go back to when I was too young to read, when I was going around to banquets and groups my parents belonged to and reciting poems in Yiddish. That's how I began. I don't think they ever thought I would be an actress. Later on when I said, "I'm going to go to college and study to be an actress," they were aghast, because "only whores are actors," you know, and ne'er-do-wells of other sorts.

I danced a little, and I did radio in Philadelphia at station KYW. My high school did not have a drama club, so I didn't do any plays in high school. But when it was time to go to college, I was very clear: I would go to Syracuse University, which was the only school I'd heard of that had a drama school.

The drama programs were quite different in those days. There were no singing or dancing classes; it was much more academic. So I had much more of a grounding in theatrical history than I had in technique. I think the theater department was run without kindness, which essentially was actually kind, because when you tried out for parts, if you didn't get them, you didn't get them. Just because you were a senior or whatever didn't mean you got a part—just like the business. And it was run quite harshly from that point of view. I don't know that that's right, but it certainly wasn't a shock for me when I came to New York. I'd already experienced that kind of feeling.

Did you come to New York then, after you left Syracuse?
Well, my parents had offered me a car as a graduation gift, and I asked for the money instead and used it to spend the summer in Europe. It was the most glorious thing I could ever have done for myself. Then I came to New York and started to make the rounds. And in those days, you could really make rounds—that's how it was done. You made rounds to agent's offices and producer's offices. You'd sit around in the producer's office, and the producer would eventually come out and look around, and he'd say, "I don't need any of you, except maybe you, the short one over there in the corner." And then he'd clear his office and everyone else would go out. Television was just burgeoning at that point, and you'd go around to the casting people who did that and drop your pictures off and try to talk to somebody. There were only a few trade papers in those days, and you would mostly hear about things from other people.

In many ways, it was all more accessible then. Now I wouldn't be able to get into a producer's office at all. And in truth, the casting situation is very different now, because we have casting directors. There was no such thing in those days—there were only agents and producers. A couple of the really big producers had people who were on staff as casting people—David Merrick, for example, who was *the* producer in my day. But most of them would just come out of their office, look around, and pick someone, just by look. *Then* they'd look at the picture and résumé.

It feels to me like it was simpler then. My perception of it is that in those early days, there was the play, there were the people who did the work of getting it on, and there was the audience. Now there seem to be many, many more people who have made themselves necessary to get the play on. Then, there was just the producer and the director. Some of the big stars had agents, but a lot of them only had lawyers, to handle the contracts. Agents became more and more significant. They were really starting to come into their own when I got to New York. And now casting directors are even more powerful, in many ways, than agents. But then they did not exist. It was in the late seventies when some of the theaters and ad agencies started having their own casting directors. Before that, a producer for a commercial or whatever would call a couple of agents, the agents would send some people, and the director would look at them, and that would be it. I guess it just wasn't efficient, so they started getting their own casting directors. But the independent casting directors are the most powerful creatures in town now, I'd say, and they've really proliferated.

How do you feel about marketing yourself as an actor?
It's probably the hardest thing in the world to do. Maybe for some people it isn't, but I feel strongly that I'm not at all alone in how I feel about it. On the one hand, you're supposed to have sensitivity in order to be able to perform. On the other hand, you've got to have a hide of iron in order to withstand rejection.

It seems to me that I'm a very good salesperson. When I'm selling a product or telling someone how great somebody else's work is, it's easy. But for me to call someone up and say, "Hi. I'm Anita Keal. I'm a brilliant actress, I'm a beautiful woman, I'm intelligent, talented, and wonderful, and you'd better see me or you're really going to lose out," it's absolutely impossible for me to do. For one thing, it's hard to believe that inside, and yet that is what you must sell.

I can recall an interview with a new agent many years ago, and at the end of it she said to me, "I had you in, Anita, because I've seen your work, and you're a very talented actress, you're a beautiful woman, and you have a great voice and a stunning figure. But you're not really sure of yourself, and I can't trust that when you go into an audition you won't goof, that on a day when you're feeling negative about yourself, you won't read well. I had you in because I've seen your work, I've seen you in all these wonderful things and I was thinking: Why aren't you a star?" I was about 32 at the time. She said, "You should be a star, but you're not. What's wrong with you that you're not?" And now I know: It's the insecurity. It was a pretty devastating moment.

If you can somehow get hooked up with a good agent who believes in you, then he or she can do the selling for you. There are some people I know who've been with certain agents for practically their entire careers—agents who have had faith in them whether they've worked or not and would sell them, really sell them. But that's rare. If you're not signed to an agent who will do that for you, that means you're not getting a crack at decent work.

I'm with an agent now, and in the last six months, I've been up for regional theater, showcases, and minor shows. In 1978, I was earning a lot of money as a regular on a soap opera, I had just done a Broadway show and was about to do another, and while working on the soap I had done an Off-Broadway show, and if you had told me then that my career would be where it is now, I would have said, "Come on, now that I've done these things, it'll never go downhill again." But that's just not true.

I go to auditions now for things where I've read the script and I've said to my agent, "Do you really want me to read for this? This is not such a good play, and that part is stinky." My agent says, "Anita, just go." So I say to myself, "Okay, he's right. Who else is asking me to do anything?" And when I go, there are older ladies who have been stars, and some who are definitely semi-names, at that same audition! For a bad play, and not a really great role! When I see that—and I think I started seeing that five or six years ago—it tells me that there's generally a lot less work than there used to be, and there are a great many more roles for men than for women. They're not writing interesting roles for women past a certain age. A 65-year-old man can be a sexy hunk, but a 65-year-old woman is a doddering, over-the-hill grandmother. I choose not to be bitter—I believe there's no point in being bitter because it gets you nothing—but there's not a heck of a lot of work out there. What I try to do is accept what work is coming my way and do whatever appeals to me. If I really think it's awful, I won't do it.

Is there anything in particular you do between shows to keep your spirits up?

The best thing is to have a project waiting in the wings, so that when you close a show, you have something you can't wait to get back to. I do some writing, which I enjoy because then I have the ability to control the artistic end of it. You can write or take a class you've wanted to take—whatever is the next thing that you want to do.

Writing with another person is good, because then you have some structure. It can be difficult to self-motivate—nobody but you cares if you finish it. When you're rehearsing a play, somebody says, "Rehearsal is at 10 o'clock on Monday, and we're going to work Act I. Everybody have your lines learned." Somebody is telling you what to do.

But just to have something, so you can say, "Oh, good! Now that the show is closed, I can get back to that," or finally learn tatting or whatever—you go on with your life.

Do you have any advice for actors just starting out in the business?
The first thing is to look deep within yourself and find out if you really have to do this. If there is anything else in this world that you can do fairly well and enjoy, go do it. It's too difficult a business—there's too little reward. I'm also talking about stars, people who do make it: I have a good friend with whom I started out who's become a major movie star, and I see him every once in a while when he's in New York—and he is not a happy person. Succeeding or not succeeding is not always what it's about. What's important is getting satisfaction out of what you do.

I also think that, in addition to acting classes, singing classes, waiting tables, and all the other things you do starting out, you really have to get a sense of who you are. When I go to an audition that matters to me, I do all the work beforehand—I study the script, plan my actions, plan what I'm going to wear, do all that work. But in the hour or so before I go, what I work on is how I really feel about it, who I really think I am, to have some sense of my own value and to know that I'm going to be the most wonderful person in the world. I can't change who I am, and I wouldn't want to. If I'm having a bad day, then I admit it to myself. If I'm having a good day, I go with that. I think my work is more honest that way, because I'm not trying to cover up what's really going on inside, trying to look happy when I'm not, or whatever. So I don't try to be something I'm not. All I can do is be the best me I can be.

JOHNNY KLINE

Johnny Kline was born and raised in Springfield, Ohio, and earned his bachelor's degree from Goddard College in Plainfield, Vermont. At New York University, he studied in the graduate acting program. He lives in New York City.

What were your beginnings as an actor?
In south-central Ohio, where I come from, it's primarily farm country. The schools I went to were extremely conservative and very unsupportive of the arts. I was very much discouraged in terms of creative expression in the public schools.

At Goddard College, I was in a very self-reliant program, in that it's a tiny school with a tiny faculty, so we pretty much created all the theatre projects ourselves. Because of that experience, I decided I wanted to act professionally, and I went to the graduate acting program at NYU. When I got out of there, I was actually not in a position where I felt like I knew what I was doing as an actor, so then I studied with William Alderson, who was Sanford Meisner's director at the Neighborhood Playhouse for 20 years, and most of what I know now as an actor got shaped in the two years I studied with him.

Did you start "doing the business" then after you left?
Yes. Bill Alderson had a play of Horton Foote's that he wanted to direct, and there was a role in it that I was exactly right for. The play evolved into an off-Broadway production which ran for six months. Molly Ringwald and Mary Stuart Masterson played the title characters, so it created a tremendous amount of publicity, with major reviews in national publications. I got an agent from that, and met most of the casting people in the city. I got a small part in a movie with Chevy Chase and the lead in a play being done in Boston prior to opening in New York City. So I was thrust into some high-profile situations very quickly, right after getting out of acting school.

When I was playing the lead in Boston in that show, there was a fight scene at the climax of the play. I knew the fight scene had to be carefully choreographed and heavily rehearsed well in advance of opening night, but that didn't happen, and on the day we were opening, I was injured twice in rehearsal because we were still working on the fight. I had to get several stitches in my eyelid, which had been sliced open by a blade that hadn't been dulled, and I landed hard doing a 6-foot jump off a platform and destroyed some of the ligaments in my left knee. So I did the show for the rest of the run with an immobilizer on my leg. I got great reviews in two Boston papers, but a negative review in the entertainment paper in Boston that apparently carries the most weight in terms of audience size. Partly because of that, but mostly because a television actor had become interested in the role, I was dropped from the cast when the play moved to New York. It's not an uncommon story, unfortunately, but it hit me pretty hard.

I started to have some serious questions about pursuing acting in the industry. So, at that point, I stopped actively pursuing any and every opportunity that might come my way and began looking at things from a different perspective, asking myself whether a project was going to be something that I would enjoy, that I would get something out of as an actor, and that

I could use to extend my skills in the craft. I asked these kinds of questions as well of the people who were doing the casting—and so I stopped getting sent out on many auditions!

At the same time, I had enlisted Equity's help, because the company I was with in Boston had also tried to screw several of us out of some money. I made a pretty big stink about it through Equity, and Equity threatened to end the contract with the theater. So there wasn't much of a chance of ever working again with anyone who was involved at that theater, and it's possible that word had gotten around that I was a troublemaker because of that. Now I teach acting and work a lot with smaller groups of people, doing small-level shows around the city. I haven't aggressively pursued the industry since then—not that I may not again, in the future.

What are your feelings about the business?
I get very angry when I'm not accorded respect, not treated as a human being but, rather, looked upon as a commodity, as a possibility of profit for someone. And it seems that the more commercial a production is, the more actors are treated not as human beings but as cogs in a machine that's being put together to make money and further someone's, or everyone's, career. I have found that, in those commercial productions, there's a dehumanizing effect on the actor, who is, in the hierarchy of things, considered to be at the very bottom of the ladder, *unless* he or she has attained a reputation as someone who can make people money. Then there's a very different situation in terms of how they are treated.

Being as self-reliant as possible and having a very strong sense of yourself as an artist, as a person who creates art, is a tremendously empowering advantage. You can deal more effectively with the way the industry is set up, which is against the actor having that sense of self. You definitely have to have a strong enough idea of yourself that you realize that all these other people's ideas about you really have nothing to do with you personally. The massive amounts of rejection that almost necessarily come your way do not have any comment in them that has to do with you—even you as an artist. We all know people who are incredibly talented and skilled as actors but are not able to find work—because their noses are too small or whatever random thing it is that tends to leave them out of the equation. Real talent and real exciting work is often discouraged, particularly in soap operas and Broadway shows, and sometimes in Hollywood, where there's a certain formula to be adhered to which is much more important than the essence of a particular production.

Do you have any advice for actors in the business?

I think that to pursue a career in acting is probably one of the hardest things that a human being can undertake; it requires Herculean efforts. Being an artist in this society, in and of itself, is an enormously difficult task. The whole of society is actually set up to discourage that, so that's what you're up against.

Try to figure out what you need to do so that you're not taking the rejection personally. It has nothing whatsoever to do with you. You can deny the rejection; I've seen actors do it: After 14 callbacks, it's down to you and one other person who just came in on the 14th callback, and the other person gets the job because he or she is on a hot TV show or whatever, and you just say, "Oh, well, that's the breaks," and go on to the next thing. I'm not saying that you shouldn't notice the disappointment, I'm saying: Don't take it personally. It really is disappointing to be rejected, especially again and again, but it doesn't in any way, shape, or form reflect on you as a human being or on your skills as an actor.

Who you are as a person, how good you are as an artist, and how well you do in the business usually seem to be completely unrelated. Some people who are very talented happen to be making a lot of money, and some people who have little talent happen to be making a lot of money. Some people who are real jerks happen to be making a lot of money. And some people who are very talented are making no money. I kept trying to figure out the secret, thinking there had to be some formula. But the skills involved in being a good business person are just not the same skills involved in being a successful artist. They're very different skills. So there is no relationship between who you are and whether you're successful—and being able to stay clear about that is very helpful in terms of confidence.

It's a crucial differentiation to make. You can feel free to be disappointed, and can express that, without blaming yourself or feeling like you're not good enough or that you should have done something differently. There is nobody that has as much information about you as you do, and to blindly follow others' impressions of you, just because they're in some position that you're not, is never a help. The position that someone attains may have nothing to do with what he or she knows or how smart someone is.

Another thing that is tremendously helpful to actors is supporting each other fully. The industry pits us against each other in the competition for jobs, and we feel sensitive about how our career is going comparatively. It is going either better than or not as well as someone else's. These things get in the way of being able to really let each other know what it's like for us— how badly we want a certain job, how elated we feel when we get a certain job, how disappointed we are at not getting a certain job—and our insecurity about ourselves as artists. I can't think of a more powerful antidote to the emotional pains of being a professional actor than having people in your life who can really support you completely and listen to you talk about these crucial issues that we often feel alone with.

The overridingly important thing is that your life is more important than your career. There are no exceptions to that. And your life is actually a separate thing from your career. The quality of your life is not in any way dependent upon your career success, because you can actually have a very good life regardless of what stage your career attains. All you have to do is look at the newspapers to see that a highly successful career does not guarantee a good life. That doesn't diminish the importance of your career, by any means.

Being a success as an artist can be completely different from making a lot of money in the business. It's not dependent upon an external point of view but is rather a feeling within yourself. So whatever a person needs to do to move himself or herself in that direction is like gold.

I think the entertainment industry is oppressive in that it has a tendency toward pretense, of people pretending to be something other than what they are. I'm talking about people who are in a position to have power over actors and their willingness to use the enormous inequity—in terms of the number of jobs available versus the number of actors trying to get those jobs—to their personal advantage and to the disadvantage of the actors involved. Then you add the tremendous confusion surrounding what an artist is in our society, and the lack of appreciation of the importance of artistic expression, and the profound lack of respect for the artistic process in our society as a whole—and there's a great lack of that in the industry as well. All these factors melding together make for a very oppressive environment for actors, who are usually at the bottom of the heap in the entertainment industry. It's important to realize that the industry is set up rigidly; knowing that you're up against this huge complex that is not set up right is going to help you figure out how to manuever within it. You know full well that it's not your fault—it's just set up incorrectly. So an inability to get what you want has to do with the confusion within the system.

So you may be doing all the right things, in the right way, but it doesn't work because the system itself is confused?
Exactly. I think that over time, people will begin to figure out better ways of setting things up. There are some really good people out there, some really good agents who are very smart and not full of pretense, and there are

some good directors who are really intelligent and respectful about the way they treat actors. I think the numbers of those types of people will grow over time, and it'll become a much more friendly place to work and to find work. But to know that right now it's a mess and it's not set up for you—it's set up for people to make a lot of money—to know that going in is a very powerful thing.

MARSHA L.

Marsha L. was born and raised in New York City and graduated from the High School of Performing Arts, where she studied dance. She has worked on Broadway and off and in national tours. She has been a member of The Actors Studio for almost 30 years.

What made you turn to acting after studying dance?

After I'd done a couple of Broadway shows as a dancer and appeared in the first touring company of *Can Can*, I found it hard to get more work as a dancer. I was also told that I was really too short. So I decided I wanted to act.

I then studied with Nola Chilton for about four years, and I did a couple of terrific plays, including an amazing production of *Dead End* with Dustin Hoffman and Ron Liebman. I felt that some of these actors had a connection that I didn't have. I couldn't be heard, and I couldn't be seen. It was a struggle to put myself out there, because as a dancer I was used to expressing myself just with movement. I was going to quit acting, but Ron told me to study with Lee Strasberg. I studied with Strasberg for two years and got into the Actors Studio, where I've been a member for almost 30 years. I did various and sundry acting jobs, including a little work in television and film. I've written seven full-length plays and seven one-acts and had one play published by Samuel French. Almost all of them have been performed in one way or another, some worldwide, though I haven't had great commercial success.

When I was 40, I started teaching, and I've been teaching for quite some time. It's something that I really love. When you get to be 40, you want to have some worth and value in this world, to make some contribution, and I was fortunate enough to start teaching. I taught at the Lee Strasberg Theatre Institute while Lee was still alive, and then when he died I went on my own. About six years ago, I took my own space and started my own theater. I teach and produce plays there.

Has your membership in the Actors Studio led to any sort of career movement, or is it more based just on the art?

Almost all the work I've gotten has been, in one way or another, through the Studio. For instance, a woman had come to observe at the Studio, and I got a call from her about a year later to audition for a show; I got the part. I also played Queen Elizabeth in a production of *Richard III* with Al Pacino in Boston, and that was because he knew me from the Studio and I got to audition. There is virtually no work I have gotten through being "sent up" by agents or going on casting calls. So the Studio has been useful artistically and creatively as well as in terms of business.

How do you feel about agents and casting directors?

When I was younger, I used to think they didn't know anything, but I've grown to have some respect for them. I know some of them have a really good sense of what works and doesn't work, or what's "off" about an actor's ability. Then there are some casting directors who went from being secretaries somewhere to being casting directors, but they don't really know anything about acting, theater, film, or anything. They just knew some actors they could call to audition.

The thing that galls me terribly is that they get billing over actors in films, they get billing all by themselves. That just drives me up the wall when I see that! I know they work hard—I assisted a casting director on casting a film—but it's nothing compared to the creative process that the actor goes through. I think that agents have a hard job—there are a number of agents that have really liked my work, but they didn't know what to do with me. And they're in a bind, I appreciate that. There's a market out there, and they have to try to fill that market, but there's a limit to what they can fill it with.

How did you make the decision to start your own theater company?

Through teaching. I had a number of students who were very good, and I wanted to do a production with them. Then, in the place I was renting to teach, a woman directed a play of mine. She had auditions, and I suggested a number of my students to audition, and she cast all of my students in it. It was great, and I thought, "Why don't I do this?"

Well, I didn't have a space, and the cost of renting a space is really high. The woman cancelled the last week of the play because she got angry with one of the actresses, and I thought, "If I had my own space and directed something myself or had other people I know direct it, then nobody could do that to me." I'd have the artistic control. So, on a whim, I asked the super if there were any other spaces in the building, and there was one. I had rarely taken chances on anything, least of all anything economic. I had rarely had a great deal of faith in anything I might do, and it was a scary proposition. I talked to my therapist about it, and he was encouraging. At the time, my classes were full, and I had a waiting list, so I thought, "What the hell, I'll do it!" And it worked out.

I also felt it would be an opportunity for me to do the plays I've written. I have done a number of my plays at the theater, and they've done very well. It's on a small level—I don't reach a wide public and haven't gotten much publicity—but I think we do good theater, and that's why we're here. Also, I had some students who were wonderful. They'd grown tremendously as actors, and I knew that they were, psychologically, people who would never go out there and audition. I wanted to give them the opportunity to do some acting.

So many actors have trouble with marketing. I have a very hard time with the marketing aspect of the business myself, but it doesn't mean that I'm not a terrific actress.

Do you have any advice for actors just starting out in the business?

I think it behooves young people to learn the craft, learn a technique before they put themselves out there. In order to have a career, you have to be exceptionally talented, and there aren't many actors who are. I don't know that I was originally; my talent had to be nurtured and developed through study. When I started acting, I didn't have a clue. I just went out and tried to audition for things, but I didn't know what I was doing. It was a mistake. If you put yourself out there before you're ready, those people don't forget; they remember that you auditioned and didn't know what you were doing.

My advice is: Have patience. Know what you have and what you need. Every once in a while there are some people that have it right off. They start studying with me, and they could go work while they continue to study.

Do you think it's a difference in individual psychology, or just basic talent, or something else?

The people who are ready to work even if they've never studied are people who are not "hidden"—they don't have a very hidden personality. They're willing to expose, they're readily able to put themselves right out there, on one level or another. They may have some secrets, but basically, they're just not afraid.

Then you have other personalities, and I was like this, who are very hidden. I was frightened; I felt totally inadequate, like a nobody. It took working with Lee to discover that I am somebody, and that even feeling like a nobody is of value if I'm willing to let that be seen.

As an actress, I reached a point where I was able to come out of hiding, and that's what I think makes me a good actress. But I still have problems dealing with the business community. My own psychology is such that I lose the sense of my self-worth when I feel that I'm going to be judged. I go into automatic "I'm not sufficient, I'm not what they want." It's different sometimes with people who know me, and I know they know me; I'm a bit more comfortable with them, because they know me as an actor and have asked me to audition. I usually get the part then, because I know they already have something to measure me against. But when I'm auditioning for people who don't know me, I seldom get the part, and it's because of that psychology.

In addition, it can be rough because sometimes I can be very full in my acting and will go way out on a limb—I really put myself out there—and sometimes the people I audition for just don't know what to make of it or, for whatever reason, don't want to deal with it.

I have a student now who is very self-conscious. She doesn't know herself, and she thinks she's ready to work. She's impatient, and I'm sure it shows when she auditions. Some people can act all over the place and indicate, and they do it well. She doesn't do it well, which probably suggests that somewhere underneath all that is a tremendous talent. Very often that is the case.

But, for whatever reason, it's hidden or protected?
Yes. The only other thing I would say is that if you can't get out there and do the business part, so that you are a working actor, then you have to create your own thing. Find some way to do it, because that creative spirit is so important.

Try not to judge the value of what you do as an actor; try not to say, "Oh, but I'm not on Broadway." I battle with that all the time. I have to remind myself that I am acting—it's what I want to do. I write also, and I direct, but I like to act. So I do it in front of an audience of 40 people instead of 400 or 4,000. For me, that's better than not doing it at all. It's satisfaction for me, and it's satisfaction for the audience.

As a director, how do you work with actors and communicate or connect with them?

I communicate as a director very differently from the way I communicate as a teacher. As a director, I want results, certain end results. I direct the way I like to be directed. I want to say to directors: "Tell me what you want, and I'll get there. Don't tell me how to get there, just tell me what you want, and let me get there."

I also try to work with actors in relation to what they're capable of. I may want something, but at a certain point, as a director, I have to be able to see if I'm not going to be able to get it. And if I can't, then I have to use the best of what that person is capable of and use it fully, whether it's true or not true—good, bad, or indifferent. If an actor is having trouble giving me what I want, he or she is pretty much stuck. The actors that come up with a million different things are easier to work with, because then I can pick and choose. That's usually what I want as a director, to have an actor bring me something—something truthful, real, and dimensional, not just an idea or a convention, which I can read on the page. Sometimes I have to settle for the obvious, if that's all the actor can bring me. But what I really want is the human being, the uniqueness of the actor.

MARTHA M.

Martha M. grew up in Tennessee, and trained at the University of Tennessee and at Northwestern. In New York, she studied under Uta Hagen and at the Neighborhood Playhouse and took various professional courses ranging from auditioning to vocal training.

What made you originally choose to be an actress?

I just was one. That's just who I was. We were doing an operetta in school, and a friend of mine went to audition for it. She asked me to go with her, and I ended up getting a part. So I had to learn all the lines, and all the songs. It never occurred to me that I didn't necessarily have to do it. And I remember the director watching the show one night in the wings and motioning to me onstage, trying to get me to move downstage—I think because my voice was not projecting. And so I moved down, and afterwards he came up to me and said, "You didn't break character—you moved right downstage, you followed directions, and you didn't break character. You're a born actress!" It was the first time somebody told me I was something. I knew what he was talking about, and though I didn't really understand it, I felt comfortable in a way that wasn't familiar to me. I really enjoyed it.

Why did you decide to leave the business?

The circumstances in my life changed. I was getting a very favorable response from my work and things were going well, but the statistics show, and the realities are, that it is hard. You work as a waitress, you do things to keep your life going. The circumstances changed in my life so that I felt that both emotionally and financially I needed more security, at least during that period. It was very, very, very difficult to decide to do it.

A good friend of mine who was very successful in commercials had called me about a year before and said, "Can we go to lunch? I just want to talk." He was getting fed up with the business and feeling that he needed more immediate feedback and a more creative challenge than the business portion of the acting profession was affording him on a day-to-day basis. He had started doing some work on the set of a John Sayles film, just getting his feet wet, and he became more and more involved in that and moved into film production and writing. So about a year later, when my circumstances changed, I thought about moving into film production. It's still theatrical, there's still acting in film, and it's still close to the thing I love, which is storytelling. And I knew someone who had moved into it. So I called him and said, "Okay, it's time for you to take me to lunch now." I was in the process of deciding to segue into another entertainment field, develop other techniques and business skills, and support myself in a more secure fashion. Also, I wanted more control over my life. Those were my reasons.

And I found the concept of having control exciting. I felt there were more doors that I could draw open faster. In fact, it almost felt as if there were too many doors, in a way, compared to the acting profession. There was such a difference! And I was excited about being able to move at a faster pace and getting the feeling that if I were to bite it off and chew it, there was something there waiting for me.

But it was so hard. And the final thing, I think, was that I realized that acting had always been my identity. Even though I was able to create other things, I realized that everything I knew about myself or had hooked myself onto, every term I used to describe myself, all centered around one thing: this profession. And I didn't know what to do about it. I had given up the other things I had wanted in order to pursue my career, and I didn't know what to do about that.

Now I feel that a whole community of people who are dear, dear friends don't know me. Or as much as they do know me, they've never seen me perform, and most of them don't even know that I did perform. I've been doing this other work for about fifteen years, and there are people, especially younger friends that I have now, who say, "What? You're kidding!" when I mention offhand that I was in the theater. And I truly believe they're not seeing me, and that there is something in me that is not coming through, even in my personality—it's just sitting there waiting. A friend of mine whom I've known for many years recently saw me perform again, and he said there was something that's just different about me, something that doesn't resonate in the same way.

The other reason I left, which is probably the core issue, was that, initially, learning a technique had sort of freed me up in a very exciting way, and then suddenly it was becoming very, very frustrating. I realized that I'd gotten to the point where I had to grow as a person, I had to face some deep issues, and I didn't even know what they were. I wanted to be a very truthful actress, rather than representational, and to put everything I was into a character; I wanted my work to really be "in the moment" and with heightened stakes. And I found that I was having a lot of difficulty doing it, because I would have to know what the character thought and step into it emotionally, but I didn't even know what *I* thought. It sounds so trite, but I didn't know who I was.

I was 28 when I came to New York, and I'd lived a whole other life. I couldn't have put it that clearly at the time, but I remember getting out of a taxi and realizing that it was more important for me to make the taxi driver happy than it was for me to be me. I was shocked at how hard I had worked so that he would have a nice ride! I remember thinking, "How can I play a character well when I don't know what I'm thinking or who I am?" Looking back on it, I knew on some intellectual and emotional level that I was going to have to find out who I was.

I didn't think I could live as an actor during that period. I didn't know how long it would take—maybe a year, or three or five—but it would have to go on however long it went on, and I don't think I could have put up with the business while I did it. There would have always been something I had to do about going to auditions or getting into a show, and it would have driven me crazy. Now, I'd like to think that somewhere inside I knew it was a long process and that I had to have more feedback and experience. It would not have helped to continue auditioning.

After all those years, when I did go back to do some performing, it was exactly what I wanted it to be. The first steps were very, very scary, but the reward was incredible. And it was life experience that made the difference. Now I can do it the way I want to do it.

Any advice for actors just starting out in the business?

While you've got your parents' money to help you do it, find another way to support yourself. And think really smart—find something that is always going to be there, with maximum dollars for the amount of effort, that you can do anytime, day or night. Whether it's word processing or giving massages, something that you like doing, it will give you some support. I know an actress who is pretty much in my situation now, trying to find a way to get back into a more arts-related and yet secure position. She's going back to train so that she can teach. If you can do that while you're training to do your dream, that would be best. Maybe you'll find out, through working with a caterer, that you really enjoy food preparation. I know someone who is a brewer of beer. You could be a wine steward, if you really like that, and at a good restaurant you could really make bucks and still get up in the morning and go to auditions. Find something so that you can go for your dream and train for it, but so that you also have something else you like just as much.

The soul of an artist can really get beat up doing a lot of the different kinds of work that artists have to do, and after about four or five years of doing it, if they're doing a lot of menial things, they don't feel good about themselves. They still don't have any money, but their friends who are younger and not in the business are starting to think about buying a co-op. Or they're dealing with an agent who's some jerk who has no idea who they are—all those things can happen to you, and meanwhile you still have to do what you do—go to auditions.

You have to feel secure. Don't let your dream talk you out of finding something to make money, something separate, but that you still like.

In terms of your dreams and fantasies, some carrot has got to be out there. If it's a picture of you accepting an Academy Award, so be it. Whatever it is, you have to have it, and you can't let life take it away from you, no matter how difficult it gets. You're the only person who can take it away or compromise on it.

You have to have a fantasy. There's a fine line between working to achieve your fantasy and living your real life, too. You don't want reality to hurt your dream, and you don't want your dream to hurt your real life. You have to realize that your dream may take a lot of work. One of my best friends now has a television show, a Tony, an Emmy, and a contract for a major film part; he's been on Broadway, is financially set, and is starting his own production company. It's a name that everybody would know if I said it. He has always worked, pretty much, and is incredibly talented. But it took him 25 years to get where he is.

There are a lot of different realities. Getting in touch with those realities is a practical and very important thing to do, and it doesn't have to destroy your dream. If you can figure out ways to pay your bills and to learn your technique, then you can do it. Don't just give up your dream, and throw it away, to do what you have to do to survive. Dreams can be very fragile and can get wiped out. It's your dream, nobody else's—you need to protect it. Don't give it away.

ANNE V. SAWYER

Anne V. Sawyer grew up in southern Florida and started acting when she was 11. In New York City. She studied at NYU and at the Lee Strasberg Theatre Institute. Anne is now a writer, and her plays have been published and produced in New York City.

How did you go about pursuing your desire to become an actor?
When I was young, all my friends were going to this neighborhood children's theater group run by a woman who had been in several Broadway tours. I was fairly shy, and my family was kind of repressed—we had the semblance of a normal family, but it wasn't as normal as it looked. The acting really gave me an outlet.

The first show we did was *Free to Be You and Me,* and I did a song, but I was too shy to sing, so I spoke most of the part. It was really exciting for me. My parents came, and the woman who ran it told them how great I was and kissed me, and that was just the beginning. After three years, I realized I wanted to be an actress, so I decided, all on my own, that I needed headshots. My parents didn't push me or motivate me. We had a family friend who was a photographer, and she did a bunch of shots, and I picked one. I went to an agency, and they sent me on an audition, and I got the part, right off the bat. It was the pilot to a series for a children's after-school special. I got into SAG that way, which was great. I was only 14 and was already in the union. I just kept up with it through high school, and when I decided to go to college, all I wanted to do was be an actress and move to New York.

I was at the Strasberg Institute for a year, but it was horrible. I got C's in acting, because with the Method, they don't tell you the intellectual aspect of it, you just have to do it. I wasn't in the right "space" to learn that way. I ran out of money, so I worked and tried to audition, and I eventually had to move back to Florida for a couple of years.

I auditioned in Florida, and there they're called "bikini auditions"—you literally wear a bikini, and you're put on videotape. I got a co-starring feature film role in *The Heavenly Kid.* And I thought that when the movie came out, producers and directors would start calling me and I'd get work. But they held it for summer release, and it came out the same week as *Back to the Future* and *Weird Science,* so it totally flopped. The other actress in the film moved to New York and was taking an acting class and auditioning for soaps. I moved to New York, moved in with her, and she got a soap and I didn't. I temped, and she kept auditioning and got a lot of work.

So the reasons you chose acting were that it was fun, and you felt accepted?
I could express myself, I could get attention, and it was a lot of fun. It made me feel special. Now that I don't act anymore, I miss the fact that no matter what you're doing up there, as long as it's honest and you've done your homework—made your choices, worked on it—and you're relaxed, it's going to work. People are going to like it, and you'll get satisfaction at the same time.

How did you make the decision to stop acting?
It was a very gradual decision. I thought for a long time that if I ever had to give up acting, I'd feel humiliated and feel like a failure. And being in psychotherapy and starting to write really helped me make the transition.

It wasn't so much that I stopped—I just did it less and less. It didn't meet the same needs for me anymore. When I was a kid, I hadn't had any ambivalence about it as a choice. But when I came back to New York and started auditioning, my agent said, "You should change your hair color; it doesn't look natural"—I was a bleached blond at the time—and that kind of thing devastated me. Instead of receiving it as business advice, I really took it personally. It made me feel like I wasn't good enough.

Auditions became very difficult—plus having to work for a living all the time. I enjoyed acting classes, but I didn't have the internal ability to deal with the rejection of the business, because it just felt so personal to me.

Now that I'm a writer, I'm not as dependent on external reinforcement. I write something, I send it out, and if I send it to twenty places and they all reject it, I don't care. It's done. It's intrinsically valuable, and I don't need anybody else's validation to know it. Whereas with acting, if somebody doesn't like you or give you a part, you're powerless. And a lot of people in the field—actors and people in power positions—have their own issues, and that can really screw you up. I had a situation with an agent in which I started crying right in front of him because he was so rude to me. I was nervous, and I was leaning forward, trying to look interested, and he said, "Get your elbows off my desk! Sit back and cut the attitude!" Now that I'm a few years older, I probably would say something back to him. But then I was young and insecure, and I wasn't smart enough or in a position to do that. I don't know if this applies to a lot of people, but it's taken me a long time to realize that if somebody doesn't like one thing about me, that doesn't make all of me unacceptable.

It's just a crazy field; it's ridiculous in a way. I know a lot of actors who are really, really good and don't get work. And I didn't want to turn around in ten years and say, "Wow, still temping!" Look at Danny DeVito—look how long he struggled. I mean, everybody struggles like hell! And for me, I couldn't do it. It was just too much.

Acting served a good purpose for me. When I was younger, it did gratify me. And it made me who I am. But I was crazy for acting—I read biographies, autobiographies, plays, everything in the damn library. It was like an addiction.

I used to go to those open calls at Equity. You'd have to get there at 6 or 7 in the morning to sign up for an audition a week later. I'd get there at 7 AM, and there would already be a line outside in the freezing cold. That's one of the things that made me decide to stop acting. There are people who get up at 3 AM and drive in from Pittsburgh so that they can get a number and come back in a week. Sometimes people wait all that time and then don't even get a number. It's ridiculous. Why don't you just live outside and flay yourself every day instead? It's such a hard thing, and there's so little support.

Do you have any advice for people who are thinking of getting out of the business, but can't quite make the decision yet?
You really need to assess what it is you want. If you want to be an actor, there's nothing wrong with that. There are some really good actors out there. But you have to have a life, too. I know actors who feel that acting is

their whole life—auditioning and more auditioning—and everything's tied up in that. They're living in awful apartments and they haven't really started their lives yet. You need to have ways to take care of yourself and nurture yourself in other areas. And you have to have a very realistic sense of the business, an objectivity about the business aspect of it. You have to be able to go to fifty auditions and, if they don't like you, just not care. For me, it was so tied in with how great it was when I was a kid and what it meant then that I couldn't *not* care.

There's nothing fair about it, and there's no guaranteed reward—I wanted a guarantee. If you need a guarantee out of it, don't do it. If you don't care, if you can be happy just auditioning and doing whatever work you can get, great! Keep doing it! You may never get famous—who cares? If you love doing it, then that's not going to matter.

Now I have a much better sense of what life as a successful working actor would be like than I did when I started—I don't know if I even had any clear sense of it. It's much different from what I had imagined. I know an actor who played a fireman on a pilot for a TV show, and when they decided to create an actual show from the pilot, he auditioned and auditioned and got called back and got called back, but he didn't get it. And that happens over and over and over. It's just a really hard business.

Is there anything specific that you think actors just starting out in the business should know?

That it's first and foremost a business; that you need to study with someone who's good, who can nurture your ability and talent. I've seen teachers who yell at their students or degrade them in front of other students. You don't have to buy into that.

You should be realistic about the way you look. You can't make yourself look much different from the way you are. Be realistic about your headshots—nobody's expecting you to be Laurence Olivier. Be yourself, be honest and straightforward, and be proud of who you are.

It's important to have technique so that you know what you're doing. It's not some mystical power. Some actors go into the business with the idea that it gives them a license to screw around with their lives: "Oh, I have to live a tormented existence, and I can't be organized, and I can't be functional." And that's totally wrong. You don't have to live in chaos, you don't have to go out and get drunk all the time or live on the ragged edge of survival to be an actor. You need to get some structure for yourself, because that makes it easier.

Also, a lot of actors are afraid that if they go into therapy, it will rob them of their creativity, that the things that make them screwed up are the things that make them interesting, that fuel their acting ability. The fact of the matter is, you don't lose it, you don't lose any of the experiences that you draw on, you just have better access to them. And then they don't screw up your normal life.

It's hard, when you're doing a role, to separate yourself from the character at the end of the evening and not carry with you all the stuff that goes with the role. If you don't have a fairly good life outside your acting and the business, you're just letting yourself in for a hard time.

MICHAEL DAVIS SUTTON

Michael Davis Sutton grew up in Radford, a small town in southwest Virginia. A standup comedian and a dancer for many years, he is now a writer and lives in New York City.

What was it like coming from the Southern countryside to New York to be a performer?
Radford was very rural, very religious. I had a poor kind of upbringing in a large extended family. My father worked in a factory, my mother worked at K-Mart and in different dress shops. We all went to the little red schoolhouse down the road. It was very much like *The Waltons*.

I was really small for my age, and when I was in high school the drama teacher asked me and a friend of mine to audition for *Carousel*. I thought he recognized my talent and wanted me to audition, but it turned out that they just needed actors to play kids. But my parents wouldn't let me go to rehearsals, because it was too much "fretting around," too much trouble. So I didn't get to do it, and I was really miserable.

In my junior year, I auditioned for *Dark of the Moon,* and I got the part of Preacher Haggler. Once again, my parents weren't excited that I'd be having to run up to the school every night. But by this time I had friends who had cars, so when I told my parents that they wouldn't have to take me or expend any energy whatsoever, they let me do it. I was extremely excited and had lots of fun at rehearsals. The director always yelled at me a lot, and I always thought I was horrible. But it was just so much fun to be out of the house and doing something.

When I came onstage in that show—I had to walk across the stage to start my scene, and I had a little walk that I did—people started to titter, and by the time I got to the other side, they were really laughing. And with every line I said, people laughed. People kept coming up to me later and saying, "Michael, you were hysterical!"

The show got good reviews, and in the next few weeks of school, people that would never have talked to me otherwise—football players and people who were in other classes or "out of my league," as my parents would say—would tell me how funny I was in the play. That was a wonderful experience.

The next show was a one-act, and there was a big one-act competition statewide. I really wanted to do that, because it meant three overnight trips—district, regional, and state—so I could get out of the house. I *lived* to get out of the house. I told my parents that I was going to audition for it, and they said, "You most certainly are not. We're sick of this running around, and we ain't putting up with it." My parents were just control freaks; everything was, "I don't think you need to do that" or "I don't really think that's necessary." *They* don't do anything, and they expected their kids not to do anything. But I wanted to do this. For one thing, somebody wanted me and asked me to audition. People wanted to be around me, and my friends were saying, "It won't be any fun unless you're in the play." I had never felt wanted by my family; I felt like a burden for many different reasons, and being wanted felt good.

More than anything, I wanted to go away to school, but my parents had no money and told me I had to win a scholarship in order to go to college. And I thought, "One more year in that house, and somebody's going to take a gun and blow somebody's head off." In my senior year, there was a serious play that, of course, I was *not* in, that was going to a competition where you could compete for an acting scholarship—first, second, or third place. I asked if I could tag along and compete. I worked on the material for two months before the competition, and every night I literally prayed I would get it. I knew I wouldn't get one based on my grades. So I competed, and I thought I didn't have a chance because there were great-looking people and Shakespearean actors involved. And I won the first-place scholarship! Everybody kept saying, "I can't believe it!"

I went home, and my parents would not believe that I had won the scholarship. I had to get someone else to tell them before they believed it. This is how much faith they had in me. So I got to go away to college.

People said I should be a standup comic because I was so funny. I think pursuing acting had a lot to do with the fact that it was an area where people wanted me and were asking me to join them, and that I was the funniest of the group.

I came to New York on a Greyhound bus with $600 in my shoe. And I dragged two friends with me. When I first got here, it was thrilling. I took classes at HB Studio and dance classes, and I worked very hard. I never had an agent as an actor. I never pursued the business aspect of it even half as hard as I should have, and I kind of regret that. I auditioned sporadically, and I never really marketed myself. Auditioning always made me very nervous because I kept hoping they'd want me.

At that time, a friend of mine who was doing a cabaret act at a club asked me to be his opening act. He said, "You're the funniest person I have ever met." It struck a chord in me, and I knew I had to do it, because so many people had told me I was funny. The first night I did it, I got a standing ovation. The manager of the club asked me who my agent was. He basically told me I was going to be a star and asked if he could book me for an hour show. So I stopped auditioning and started working on my comedy. I did standup comedy for about four or five years, got an agent, and toured the country.

I had written my own material as a comic, and when I got back to New York I realized that I didn't want to go back into that frightening world of auditioning. I didn't have any other artistic outlet, so I started writing because there was nowhere else to put that creative energy.

Why did you leave comedy?
I actually was going up the ol' comic ladder, and my dream of all dreams was to have a sitcom, like Jerry Seinfeld or Paul Reiser. I knew that I wouldn't be seen and noticed just doing auditions, doing monologues; that wasn't showing the funny me. Somehow I couldn't get it to come out in auditions. So, like a lot of other people, I figured I'd do standup comedy to break into movies and TV and the "big time."

I really do believe that if I had kept going, I might have been able to do it. But touring was just repugnant to me. Also, having to be funny for strangers in strange towns at 11 at night, when I was tired, was very hard. It's an insular life: You're traveling the country by yourself, and you have no home. I did it for three or four months, and it was depressing. I couldn't do it. I saw it for what it was and gave it up gladly.

How do you feel about having your plays produced?
To have your play produced is a fabulous feeling. But what a mixed bag! I had one of my plays, *Blind Spot*, done as a reading with people who had won Tony awards, and they were very good. It was the best performance I think it could ever have. Then I had it produced by a regional company,

and they did a good job. But it's hard when you've seen your work in the absolutely best light, being served to the fullest capacity, and then to watch it not live up to your expectations.

To be produced is a great honor. As an artist sometimes I'm very hard on myself, because I want the production to be the very best it can possibly be, and we don't always get that.

Do you think the way you were brought up influenced your perceptions of the business?

My parents had taught me that to say you're good at something is the worst evil you could do. Pride was terrible, even to the point where, if someone complimented you on your clothing or whatever, you had to put it down and prove that it was shabby. They taught me religiously that I should not get out of my league, and that if people said I did something well, they were just trying to be nice. There was a lot of "Who do you think you are?"

When I left college, they thought I'd get an amazingly high-paying job just because I'd gone to college. I told them I was going to move to New York, and my mother said to me, "Well, just who do you think you are?" I said that I thought I was just an average guy who was going to move to New York. Her perception was that we were country bumpkins who could never get anything, and that stuck with me, and the insecurity made me very nervous for auditions. If I had listened to the outside world instead of my parents, I would have been fine. But it was all that stuff from my parents that seeped inside of me. I was told by them that I didn't need to do things, and even when they'd come to see my plays, they'd come backstage and say quickly, "Well, that was good, are you ready to go home?" while everybody else was doing the regular stuff like giving me flowers, kissing me, and saying I was great. It was an embarrassment to them, because I was "making a show of myself"—letting people say that I was good at something and thanking them. My parents just believed in putting yourself down.

Most of the time when I was auditioning, I felt as if my parents were on the other side of the table. I saw everyone in the business as being as judgmental as they were. I always had a feeling that one of the casting people or agents were going to see in me what my parents saw in me, and I was afraid that that was the real me. I was afraid that somebody would stand up in the middle of an audition and say, "You have no right to be here. What are you doing here?" I kept hearing my mother's voice saying, "These people aren't going to hire you."

You felt that the person defined by your parents was the real you, and that the one defined by the outside world was not?
Yes. Unfortunately, about 60 percent of the cells in my body believe what my parents told me, and only 40 percent believe that I'm a funny and talented person who could make it. Parents have to be "right"; they're like gods when you're young, the ones that feed you and seem to have the power of life and death. So if they say that what you're doing is stupid and unnecessary and that you're not talented, you believe them.

I had a monologue published several years ago in a book called *Moving Parts*, with Neil Simon and all these other people, and I was very excited about it. I took the book home to show to my family, and they said, "Well, I'll be darned," flipped through it real quick, and set it down on the table. But no one read it—nobody in my family picked it up and read it.

I was heavily criticized as a child and had very low self-esteem, and I thought that everyone else had the "clue" and I didn't. It's very odd, with that kind of a background, to go into a business where you're exposing yourself constantly. I fought against that early training so much, that message I always got that "You're never going to be anybody." But that 60 percent of me who believed my parents caught up with me at some point, and even though I was working hard, I gave out and got depressed. I lapsed into thinking they were right.

To this day, my parents have never told me I'm talented. They will say I'm funny, but that doesn't mean anything, because I've been funny since the day I was born. They can't say that my funniness comes out of an artistic soul or that's it's wonderful and creative. They don't see that it's work, or that I'm talented—they just see it as cracking jokes. Once my parents went to the opening of one of my plays, and afterward someone said, "He's so talented—you must be so proud." And my mother said, "Always have been!" I almost fell down. I'd bet a million dollars that they've said it to other people, but they have never said it to me.

I think it's just too intimate, and there's no intimacy in my family. And it's frightening to them. When I told them I was going to move to New York, they were frightened and tried to scare me: "Who would hire you? You don't know anybody. You'll never find a job." They were very careful to teach me not to stick my neck out; if you reach out too far, get too close to the fire, you'll get burned. Their whole message was, "Don't try for anything, and you'll be happier. Because if you try, you'll just get rained on." I think they were afraid that the farther I went away and the more successful

I became, the more distance there would be between me and them, and they would lose me. I wasn't going to move into a trailer in the backyard and do the dance that I had always done with them. It was frightening for me too, in lots of ways, but I've been here for sixteen years, so I was never afraid enough to go back.

EMILY T.

Emily T. was born and raised in a suburb of Kansas City, Missouri. She pursued an acting career for over 15 years in New York City.

What was it like wanting to be an actor when you were growing up in the Midwest?

I grew up in a very strict and religious atmosphere there, and I never felt like I belonged. I studied for two years at a theater conservatory program in St. Louis, but what they were teaching was discipline, and I'd already had too much of that. So I finished my B.A. at a smaller college where they taught by saying, "Create what works for you, and then we'll help you shape and mold it." That's really what I needed: the freedom to find myself and create the art in my own way. I really started to come into my own at that time. I spent several years performing and learning before I moved to New York, so I went with quite a bit of experience behind me.

What made you choose to be an actor?

It's the old story: When I was small, I put on little plays in the basement. I had some old clothes of my mother's and grandmother's, and I'd try to get the other kids to come over and do a sketch. I really liked it because I could play the princess or the witch, whatever character I felt like being. There was a lot of anxiety and tension in my family, and when I was playing these characters, I felt like I had some control over life. I could live a different life for a while, just lose myself in the character and the situation, and all my problems would fade away. I actually think acting served that purpose for me for a number of years. It took me quite a long time to get my personal life on track, because when things were going badly, I could always lose myself in a role—then my life didn't seem so bad. Not that it was awful; I just didn't know what I wanted, where I was going, or how to get there, and it was a lot easier to make decisions about a character than to make choices in my own life.

Acting helped me to feel focused. I think the main reason I wanted to be an actor was that I felt my own life wasn't what I wanted, so I was really living out who I was by doing roles, by portraying other people's lives.

How did you feel about marketing yourself as an actor?
That was always the sticky part. I really had no business knowledge, and I'd keep hearing people say, "If you're talented, and you work hard, eventually someone will notice you." So I kept waiting for that. But with the background I had, I wasn't very good at connecting with people. And that's a lot of what it takes—making a personal connection with another human being. The way the business is set up seemed very much like my past: the fear and anxiety, in terms of auditioning and being judged, and the feelings of powerlessness. You can do great work, the best you can do, but if you're two inches taller than what they're looking for, or your hair isn't the right color, someone else gets the job. It feels very arbitrary that way.

I could never get a photo I was satisfied with. I was still living with the childhood wish that I could be the "princess," the star, and then everybody would really care about whether I was okay or was taken care of, and of course I couldn't get a photo that reflected that unreal image of myself. I wanted to be a star so that people would pay attention to me. But I had a hard time believing in myself for a long time, and that made it difficult to promote myself.

How did you feel about agents and casting directors?
In the beginning, I was intimidated by them. I felt they had the ability to help me get what I wanted, but I couldn't even get their attention. So it was kind of a strange dichotomy: Here are these people who can give me what I want, but I can't get a response from them because there are so many other people trying to get their attention, too. I kept trying and trying, and over time I did get a few good roles—a little work on the soaps—but nothing would ever seem to go anywhere. Then I'd feel like I was back where I started. I was so sensitive to everyone else's appraisal of me that, if a casting director or agent wasn't enthusiastic about me after an audition, I felt really let down, like I wasn't worth anything, even as a person. Yet at the same time I knew there was this wonderful person inside of me—intelligent, strong, full of life. I could sense it. Again, a dichotomy that was very confusing to me, and I'm sure it was reflected in the way people saw me.

How long did you stay in the business?

I pursued it for a little over fifteen years, with more energy at some times than at others. I thought about leaving for a long time, because it just wasn't satisfying for me, and I was getting burned out. But it had been such a major part of my life for so long—I'd always wanted to be an actress—that I was afraid somehow that I'd have to give up my *self* if I gave up acting. I sort of "stored" all the wonderful parts of myself in the acting, which I'd bring out for this character or that, but which I couldn't really acknowledge in my own life. I could play a character who was extremely smart and courageous and play it well, but I didn't feel that way in my life. It was almost like acting was the real world, where I could be the person I was truly meant to be, and my real life was a dull mirror of it, a life I had to trudge through in order to be able to act.

Also, I was afraid to leave because I thought I'd feel I'd wasted that fifteen years of my life if I went on to something else. But it really was an incredible experience for me. Acting allowed me to explore parts of myself that I might not have discovered otherwise. It's like getting the experience of a number of lives, instead of just one, because you're playing different roles. So as I look back on it, it really wasn't a waste of time.

How did you make the transition out of the business?

The most important thing for me was dealing with all the emotional stuff I brought to the business from my childhood. It became for me an incredible replaying of all the problems I had been up against when I was small. As I got older, I found that the more I learned to face and deal with my own anger and pain, and the more I found other things in my life that I enjoyed, the less I enjoyed acting. It became, over time, something that dragged on me rather than something that fulfilled me. It had probably served as an outlet for all the feelings I couldn't acknowledge. And that probably contributed to my lack of success, because I really wasn't approaching the business in a realistic way.

It was amazing to me, as I began to pull away from the business, how many aspects of it were just like my childhood. For instance, I realized that I had a hard time promoting myself because I was taught that it wasn't nice to brag about myself. I also think a problem in the business, and in society, is that we tend not to believe people who are saying for themselves that they have talent or intelligence or whatever, but as long as *someone else* is saying, "He's really talented," or "She's really smart," we believe that someone else. It's a product of the repression in society concerning not being egotistical, not being selfish. But if you really *are* talented or smart, then it's not egotistical to say that.

It's very important to find people who support you for who you are, not just because you're an actor. There's a tremendous camaraderie among actors, and after a while you can begin to feel that if you're not enjoying acting or are not fulfilled by it anymore, there's something wrong with you—just because the people you've been friends with are actors. The interesting thing is that once I backed away from the business and tried other creative outlets, like painting and writing, the emotional baggage wasn't there for me as it was in the business. I could just paint, or write, just for the joy of creating, and I didn't worry about whether someone else would like it, or whether it would "get me somewhere." There are a lot of things I enjoy now in my life, and I think giving up the business has helped me to find a real sense of freedom in my life.

Do you have any advice for actors just starting out in the business?

First and foremost, don't expect it to fulfill your emotional needs. If you have even a sense that there's an empty place inside of you that acting will fill, take some time before you begin pursuing the business and try to figure out exactly what it is you want out of it. If you don't have a realistic sense of the business, it can eat you alive. I've seen people who were incredibly burned out after twenty or thirty years of struggling, but there they are, still auditioning and still hoping for the big break. It's a terribly difficult business, kind of ruthless in a way.

If you can put as much energy into making your life work as you put into making your career work, it can save you from investing yourself in your career so greatly that there's nothing left if you don't succeed. Having a good life is much more important than pursuing the business. I just can't emphasize that enough. Once you start to pursue the business, it takes so much time and energy that there's not much left over to build a good life for yourself, to find other things that make you happy. Reach out to that wonderful person inside you and find out what it is you're seeking from acting. Then, if you still want to pursue the business, go for it. But make sure you're not looking for your life in the business, because you probably won't find it there.

CAROLYN YOUNGER

Carolyn Younger was born and raised in Toronto, Canada, and attended the National Theater School of Canada in Montreal. She worked at the Stratford, Ontario Festival, at Cleveland Play House, at Arena Stage, and at the Philadelphia Drama Guild before moving to New York.

Do you sense a difference between the way the business worked in Canada and the way it works in New York?

Absolutely. I was not prepared for the New York environment. In Canada, I was known, and I had contacts. I'm not saying it was easy, but my age, my look, my accent, all contributed to my being in the right place at the right time in terms of my commercial look. As far as theater went, it was going pretty well until I left. When I ended up in New York, I had no clue about the business at all, because I had rarely auditioned for things—people had always come to me with jobs. So I wasn't prepared for this whole business of pursuing work. I didn't realize that almost 75 percent of what you do is the business of looking for work. It's not about doing the work, it's about getting the work. It's just overwhelming.

I remember one audition I had, for the Public Theater. I was nervous about the piece to begin with. I really didn't have good audition material, because I had never had to go through the process of auditioning. There were two people auditioning me, and when I was finished, one of them said, "Thank you very much," without even looking up. I left, and just walked and walked, with tears streaming down my face. I was devastated. I don't think I tried to audition for months after that—I was convinced that I had no business on the stage, that I was a terrible actress. I knew people who worked at the Public, and it didn't seem to me that they were so much more wonderful than I was. I felt that my audition was terrible, hence, "I must be a bad actress."

What was it that first made you want to be an actress?

I loved reciting when I was little, and I used to put plays on in the basement. I was very comfortable in front of people, and I loved performing—it was part of my nature. So it just seemed to me perfectly natural to be an actress. When I was in high school, I still wanted to be an actress, but my mother was frightened to death by the possibility. She thought the profession was filled with "bad people, perverts and such," and that there was nothing to respect about the art.

The odd thing is that she loved to go to the theater. She took me to my first Shakespeare play when I was ten years old. She loved the pageantry and, I think, secretly yearned for that. But as a mother, she wanted to protect me from that hurt and the possibly bad situations that she knew could occur. And I was pretty innocent then. I trusted everybody and would never think that anybody could do bad things. Since I didn't get any encouragement to go into acting, I thought, "Well, then I'd better do something for the good of other people." I decided to be a social worker. I went to the University of Toronto, but after three years in an honors course, I had what could be termed a little nervous breakdown. I couldn't do it. I was lost, and didn't care for the work I was doing. I was the first person in my family who had gone to college, and there are a lot of new ideas, different life-styles, different things that assault you, and my value system was sort of turned over. When I had my little breakdown, my mom asked, "Well, what is it that you really want to do?" And I said, "All I want do is theater. That's the only thing that makes me happy. It always has."

So my mother, bless her heart, sent off to the National Theater School to get some literature. I got it, made the application, did the audition, and got in. That's how I got started: My dream as a child got sidetracked with other things, but then came back.

What the theater was for me was a very safe place where I could express opinions, show some temperament, talk back, and all that, which I did not do in my family. It was a tremendous sense of freedom for me to be performing, and also to be in the profession itself. For many years, I led—I won't say a double life, but my mom likes everything to be "nice," so if I was in something a little risqué, I felt I had to hold her at a distance from my work. At some point, I realized that I should stop trying to get whatever it was that I needed in terms of support for my career from her, because she just wasn't going to be able to give it. It was a very healthy discovery.

How do you feel about marketing yourself as an actress?

When I came to New York, I was clueless about that. It took a long time for me to accept that that's what you have to do. I took some marketing courses at the Actor's Institute and the Actor's Information Project. Actors can come up with all kinds of excuses for not mailing their photos, but I think the most important thing is to just get your photos out there. What happens for me is that I get gung-ho about it, I send them out, things start to go, and then something happens and I stop. I'm not sure whether it's the burden of churning them out that gets to be too much, or interviews that I have with people that don't work out. Most recently, what has sidetracked me is that my support job, my temporary job, has become my full-time life. And after so many years, I've "run out of steam" to come home and send out photos. It's not like any other business, where you do A, B, and C, and D follows. It just doesn't work like that. I guess I want it to and get discouraged when it doesn't. And then I get depressed and stop, and then I have to start all over again.

Do you think your goal was to be "successful" rather than to be a working actor?

I believe I was a success at one time, before I came to the States. Success, for me, has a lot to do with the respect of my peers, and that I'm working with some degree of regularity. These are my prime years, and this is when I should be working. My skills are a lot better, but I'm not working. I expected, in the early years, that I would just keep on working. But that didn't happen.

The whole success thing is a really, really big issue for me, because I don't feel like a success. The weird thing is that I am probably a very successful person. People look at me, and *they* think I'm really successful as a person, but I look at myself and feel I'm not. Somehow, the fact that I don't have an agent, that I haven't done a paying theater job for years, means I'm not a success. Because I'm not a success in my chosen profession, being an actor by my terms, I therefore am not a successful human being. I am a failure.

In your whole life? Does that affect your whole life?

Yes! I'll be walking down the street, and it will come in waves over me: I'm in the middle of my life, and I'm not a success, I'm a failure. I suppose one of the reasons I kept on with my straight job for so long is that at least I didn't feel like a failure there. I could make things work and accomplish things, and therefore I wasn't a total failure. It's amazing how your whole view of yourself is tied up with whether or not you're successful in the business.

Another thing that happens to me is that after the job is over—this used to happen when I did a lot of principals in commercials—I'd go outside after people had fussed over me all day and I'd think, "Here's the real world. I'm never going to work again." I would just feel so empty inside, like something was taken away from me. I was special for a day, and now I'm not anymore.

What are your feelings about agents and casting directors?

I can be so easily intimidated, and I know the truth of it is that they don't think they're any better than we are, but because they have a certain power—they have the power to let you in or not let you in the door, to send you out or not send you out—I've had my feelings hurt so many times. When I had an agent in Canada, he was my friend. We used to sit around and drink beer together, and he'd get me a job. That was a long time ago, and he's probably out of the business by now, but there was a certain camaraderie and ease I've never been able to find here. I learned to work with somebody who liked me as a person, and who didn't see me just as an object, somebody I could just be myself with.

We're always so uncertain. You end up with this feeling that you're lacking something. You're too old, your eyes are too small, your wardrobe isn't great enough, or you don't have the right accent. Maybe you'll learn fencing, because that's another skill. Then maybe they'll like you and call you and think you have something to offer. It's always, "Let me know when you're in something"—I'm just so tired of hearing that—and then you do, and they don't come. I get so angry with that, and I don't know what else to do. You've got all this stuff, you're ready to go, and you're *good,* you can do a good job, and there's no place to take it.

Have you ever thought about giving it up, just saying: "I won't pursue the business anymore, and I'll just act wherever I want to"?

That's a tough question. I've tried thinking about myself as "not an actress," and I can't do it. It gives me panic. That's who I am, and whether I act or not, I cannot deny to myself that I am an actress and good at my craft.

Is there any advice you'd give to actors who are just starting out in the business?

I think they should take some kind of marketing course. If they're coming to New York, it would be essential. Take a course or talk to someone who offers a seminar on how to approach the business, because there's no sense in starting out making all kinds of mistakes—you're going to make mistakes anyway. Talk to someone who can help you formulate some kind of plan, so you can be methodical about it.

And get good training, because without the training you'll never really have anything to hold onto. And take classes occasionally as you go along, so you'll have a place to work when you're not getting work in the business. Have enough money when you come to get some decent headshots, or a good voice tape, or whatever you're going to need.

Finally, stay in contact with other people. It's too easy to feel isolated. Try to find a support group so you can share your experiences, and you'll find out that it's not just you that's going through this. I think that's very important.

EXERCISES TO BUILD SELF-ESTEEM

The following exercises are designed to give you some ideas about how to begin working to clear away response patterns from your childhood and negative perceptions that may be holding you back. The number-one rule in doing any work of this kind is to honor and respect any feelings that come up. Our emotions have, for many of us, been disregarded or belittled from our earliest years, so we can be quite sensitive and our feelings may be delicate.

To uncover and release your feelings, you need to give yourself time for the emotions to resurface and a place in which you feel very safe. You may have hidden your feelings for years if you were taught that they were unacceptable and disgraceful; it may have been unsafe at times for you to reveal or express them. But your feelings are basic to your humanness—the deepest expression of who you are—and they can help keep you safe by warning you of harm. Your emotions can also give you direction in terms of creating a better and more fulfilling life for yourself. Feelings that come up as you do this work are always there for a reason, even if they seem unrelated to what you're working on. If you can pay attention to them even as you experience them, you can learn why certain situations affect you so deeply.

As you first begin to explore your feelings, they may seem very intense. If you cry, you might feel as if you'll never stop. But, of course, you will stop—there is a natural ending to the re-experiencing of a past hurt, and even babies naturally stop crying after being scared or hurt if they are allowed to express their feelings fully. After a while, you'll begin to be able to build a history of your feelings, and you'll know ahead of time what situations in your present life might tend to bring up the old hurts. Then you can choose either to avoid them until you have released some of the old feelings and feel more comfortable dealing with them, or to go ahead and deal with them. Remind yourself that what's happening in the present is not the same as what happened in the past, and that you now have the adult intelligence and power necessary to deal with the situation effectively, without being hurt.

Even if you're having thoughts and feelings you don't like, you need to pay attention to them. These feelings offer a wonderful opportunity to learn about yourself, and when you try to ignore them or deny that they exist, they only become more insistent. These kinds of feelings can eventually cause you trouble because they may be ruling your behavior through your unconcious mind.

Most of us become used to having certain types of thoughts over the course of our lives. This is often a result of the ways we were taught and trained in childhood, and of our responses to this training. We tend to continue in these familiar ways, even if they might be hurtful or restrictive, rather than find a new mode of thinking and behaving that works better. If you have thoughts that are new for you, you may feel uncomfortable, but this is a part of self-discovery. Exploring those thoughts through to their very ends is an excellent way to rediscover yourself and your beliefs.

A word about so-called negative emotions: Anger, sadness, and fear exist in us all and are significant signals about our lives that can, again, help us take care of ourselves. If something in your life is making you angry, there's a reason for it. Emotions do not lie, if you are truthfully experiencing them. If the thought of a particular event or situation scares you or makes you uneasy, your feelings are probably justified. It can be either the past or the present that's affecting you. Try to tune into exactly why you're experiencing these feelings: Is someone acting politely toward you, yet you feel that person is out to get you in some way? That particular person may mean you no harm, but the fact that the feeling is there means that someone somewhere along the way probably did something to make you feel uneasy in similar situations.

When you find a thread of an idea or a possibility in your thoughts as to where a feeling might have arisen, follow it back as far as you can. See where it leads you. If you can discover and work through some of the experiences in your past which relate to the particular feelings and responses you currently have, you can often understand and resolve the situation in the present.

The important thing to remember is that these feelings arise from the most vulnerable and gentle parts of yourself, and they should always be treated with respect and love, the same way you'd treat a child who is in pain. You need to know that you can honor this vulnerable part of yourself, for yourself. Therapists and trusted friends can be an excellent source of support when you're working through difficult issues, so get help if you want or need to. But remember that you are the only one in the world who can always "be there" for yourself. Give yourself the support and care you deserve. Treat your feelings as the delicate energies that they are. You'll be rewarded in more ways than you can imagine from this work.

Remember that you are worthy of attention and respect, whether you receive it from others or not. Even if it feels silly at first, find ways to give yourself this attention and respect. Comfort yourself if you are feeling low, in whatever way seems natural: listening to your favorite music, holding a pillow, having a cup of tea or soup. If you're feeling confused or frustrated, take a few moments to figure out what's going on inside. Discover what you enjoy and bring more of it into your life. You are just as important as anyone else in this world and the only person who can discover for yourself, and give yourself, exactly what you want.

The exercises that follow should be performed only when you are alone where you won't be disturbed, or with a trusted friend or therapist. Go at your own pace and be as willing as you can to investigate any feelings and thoughts that come up while you work.

1. Use your actor's imagination: Sit in a chair facing an empty chair, and imagine a casting director/agent/producer/director sitting across from you, listening attentively. Tell him or her everything you're feeling about your audition or interview, or about your fears of meeting this person, if you haven't yet done so. Imagine this person accepting and understanding everything you say. You can even try stating how you'd like the experience to be different next time. Feel free to express any feelings that come up, in whatever way they want to be released. The point is to begin to feel that you

can establish a connection with the person, instead of seeing him or her as having all the power, and to begin to feel that you have some command of the situation, instead of feeling powerless. The more you can express the feelings that affect you strongly within a role-playing situation such as this, the less these feelings will interfere with your ability to connect with people in your auditions and interviews.

It is *not* suggested that you try this exercise with an actual agent or casting person in the business, or expect them to treat you the way your imaginary person treated you in the exercise. Agents and casting people are often overwhelmed by their own responsibilities to their clients and the people they're casting for, and by the number of actors they want to see in limited amounts of time. It's helpful to work through as many of your own patterns and perceptions as possible before meeting them in person. Having told your imaginary image what your feelings are can give you more of a feeling of command during the actual audition or interview because you've gotten the emotional entanglement out of the way. This doesn't mean using the exercise as a rehearsal for a meeting with a casting person or agent; this kind of work is only for you and should not be brought into your actual auditions and interviews. Do the work with the objective of helping yourself to grow and to discover and develop your own sense of yourself.

2. You might try the same exercise with a friend that you trust, having him or her play the role of the casting person or agent, accepting and validating your feelings as they arise. Be sure you both know that the point of the exercise is to create a safe place for each of you to express your feelings, not to have fun pretending to be a casting person at the expense of the one who is exploring certain feelings as an actor.

Be aware that doing the exercise with a friend may tempt you to repeat the process when you are in an actual audition or interview, which is not the place for this kind of work. Again, keep the work that you do on your feelings about the business and the people you meet separate from your actual dealings with those people. If you don't, you may find that people in the business would rather not be around you; they will probably find your emotions overwhelming and threatening to their own sense of self. It's fine to be open and spontaneous in an interview or audition, but expressing mostly negative feelings, or even being focused on your own feelings, will probably cause a negative reaction.

If you do this exercise before an actual audition or interview (it's best to do it more than a day or two beforehand, or you might end up carrying the feelings over into the meeting), you may find it helpful, after you've had the audition or interview, to evaluate and/or release the feelings that come up. Do this at home or in a place where you feel safe. Just knowing ahead of time exactly what you want, deep down, from a meeting with a casting person or agent can trigger memories of past events that seem similar to you in an unconcious way. (What you really want may be more than "I want them to hire me" or "I want them to sign me"—this is what this work is all about.) It helps to give yourself some time and space to express these feelings and work through the memories as they occur.

The more you can understand why certain experiences affect you the way they do, and the more clear you become about exactly what you want in a given situation, the more you'll be able to free yourself of the emotional entanglements of the past and get to a better place to achieve what you want.

3. Use your imagination again: If you could have fame as an actor, any way you wanted it, what would the ideal be for you? Millions of people knowing your name; being respected for your talents; or having people listen to what you have to say, perhaps even hanging on your every word? The answer can be a major clue to discovering yourself and uncovering neglected needs you had as a child. Take some time to sink into your fantasy, and release any feelings that come up for you. If you can find out exactly what you'd want from a successful career, you'll discover what you're looking for in your life.

Also, think about what you love about acting itself—the audience's appreciation; the intellectual stimulation of creating a character; or discovering different aspects of yourself that you can safely express, within a character, in front of people? Often what we're looking for as actors is related not only to unmet needs from childhood, such as the need for attention, but also to the need to express parts of ourselves that were frowned on when we were children.

Go ahead and spend some time indulging your fantasies: Imagine yourself in front of a wildly applauding audience, or playing Stanley Kowalski or Blanche DuBois on Broadway—whatever constituted your original dream, the reasons you went into acting in the first place. It's most important to get back in touch with what originally started you on this road as often as you can. It's so easy to lose the joy of the art, your creativity, your heart and soul, when you're working to succeed. One of the ways you can refuel your dream is by imagining that it has come true. As time goes by, and you uncover and work through more and more of your feelings surrounding the business, take care to redefine and refocus your dreams. They may change depending on where you are and how you grow. Dreams should grow with you; remember to feed them as often as you can. The more you can discover exactly what it is you want from acting and from the business, the closer you will be to getting free of your past patterns and finding ways to get what you want in every area of your life.

4. Begin to focus on discovering qualities in yourself that are outside of your "type" or family role. If you find yourself responding to an event or situation in a way that's very familiar to you, ask yourself if that's how you want to respond. Has it become a habit for you to respond in the same way to similar situations? If you discover that you'd like to respond in different ways, think about what options you might have in situations that come up frequently. For example, if your habitual response is always to say yes when people ask you to do something for them, and you realize later that you really don't want to or don't have the time, practice saying no the next time it happens. If you're not sure whether you want to or not, tell the person "I'll get back to you," and make the decision when you have a safe space in which to think about it, and then say yes or no. If the "yes habit" is particularly strong for you, you may need to begin by spending some time alone just saying "no" out loud, until you begin to feel comfortable with it.

If you have a pattern of being late to auditions or interviews, or not returning phone calls, ask yourself if you've had a pattern of procrastination in your life, perhaps even in childhood, when you put off cleaning your room or doing chores because you were angry at someone. Then practice responding outside of the pattern by returning one phone call, or making it a point to be on time one day a week.

Pay more attention to how you feel when you respond to a situation in a habitual way. It may make you feel comfortable and safe because that response kept you safe as a child in a difficult environment, but it can also limit the number of options you have for dealing with a situation. This can cause frustration and anger. Many of these kinds of habits are based on patterns of responding developed early in life as a result of imposed family roles. The more you can pinpoint them and discover their roots, the less of a hold they will have on your life and the more your ability to choose what you want, based on your current life instead of your past, will grow.

It can take a lot of practice to break habitual patterns of responding. But the rewards of connecting with your own spontaneous responses (as compared to the ones you had to develop because of a problematic family situation) will be well worth the time and attention given to moving beyond the patterns.

5. It's also important to release or discharge your feelings as they come up, as much as you can. This is an exercise to work on when you're alone or with a trusted friend or therapist. You will need some time; don't engage in this when you're close to an audition or interview, for your work can be affected. The emotions that may come up can take time to work through.

To begin, you might pay close attention to the feelings that come up when you do the first four exercises, or when you don't get a callback or role you wanted. Then try to release them in whatever way they seek expression: by crying, pounding your fist into an old pillow, waving your arms and stamping your feet, sticking your tongue out, or whatever seems like a natural expression of what you're feeling. Don't try to push something to the surface in order to make the exercise "work"; it's most beneficial if the feelings are allowed to surface on their own and release in their own unique way, without any "tampering."

Sometimes, bits and pieces of past experiences may flash through your mind as you release feelings. This is natural, and old feelings that may have been bottled up for years are exactly what you need to release in order to connect with others in the business in a more self-confident and straightforward way. Even if you feel nothing at first, keep paying attention to anything that comes up for you: These are thoughts and feelings that may have been incubating and hiding for a long time, so it may take some time and attention before you can begin to look at and release them. If you feel like you're having trouble paying attention to yourself, relaxation exercises may help: Sometimes just lying down and "listening to your body" can be a catalyst for releasing feelings.

Remember that this is, and should be, a natural process. Everyone worked this way as a baby, but our society and culture, and often our families, taught us that it was unnatural to express our feelings as we grew up. On the contrary, it's much more natural and effective to release our emotional reactions to experiences whenever we can, instead of bottling them up and stuffing them down time after time so that they pop out in unexpected and unappreciated ways at inconvenient times, or turn into illness or disease. Learn to pay attention to these feelings and release them as they come up. It seem strange at first, but that's only because we were trained so thoroughly by family and society to ignore feelings and push them away.

Respect yourself and your feelings. The more you do, the stronger your connection with yourself will become. As you go deeper into your self and release more and more of the negative emotions from your past, you'll probably find that you not only feel more self-confident and focused in terms of the business, but that your acting instrument—intelligence, creativity, body, voice, heart, and soul—will deepen and expand, and your power and ability as an actor will increase as well.

6. Another way to release some of your feelings is to turn on the radio, or put on your favorite music, and just move—roll your head, swing your arms, jump up and down, and dance. Let a feeling of freedom enter your body, and let your body move in whatever way the impulse strikes you. Put on some slow, jazzy music, and see what your body wants to do. Try the same thing with rock, rap, classical—whatever you like. Notice how different kinds of music can bring up different feelings for you. Let your intuition lead and your body follow. If a feeling comes up, and it interests you, explore it. If you want to make fists and have a boxing match with a particularly bothersome thought or belief that you discover, do it. The point in this exercise is to get your body moving so that the trapped energy can flow through you and release. Try to go along with whatever comes up, whatever occurs to you. Your body is intelligent, and in an exercise like this it can lead you in directions that might not be obvious if you're using only your mind to solve a problem.

You may find sometimes that a sense of enjoyment and fun will come over you in doing these exercises. Although one of the major purposes of this work is to discover and release negative feelings and perceptions, the real purpose behind releasing all the negativity is creating more joy and fulfillment in your life. If you suddenly feel happy while you're moving, let these feelings flow through you and enjoy them. Often, when we try to hold on to moments of happiness, they quickly disappear. The more you can let the good feelings flow through you without holding on, the more there will be. And there's no need to feel guilty. Guilt is usually just a result of having been shamed for having good feelings when you were small. Your feelings are only your feelings; they are, in themselves, neither good nor bad. So enjoy the pleasant ones when they come along.

your memory and thinking about a positive act-
, in the past. Was there a show you really loved
t, or a group you worked with that just felt exactly
different aspects of the experience to try to discover
it so wonderful for you, and imagine finding that kind
of i. gain. If you can differentiate the kinds of roles or groups
that are u. t enlivening for you, you can seek out those elements and
look for ways to re-create those enjoyable experiences. You'll refine your
sense of the kind of work you like and the people you most enjoy being
with.

8. Journal writing is one of the easiest ways to express your feelings. The key
to this practice is to be completely nonjudgmental about what you're writing *as* you're writing. Just let your thoughts and feelings flow onto the page.

If you have trouble getting started, try filling in the blanks:

"What I'm feeling right now is _____."

"I felt _____ about my last audition, because it was _____ for me."

"The childhood experience that most deeply shaped me as an actor was
_____."

Whatever your mind wants to set on the page is fine. The freer you can
become in expressing yourself in a journal, the easier it will be to know
quickly how you're feeling about a situation. It can help you to feel that
someone is "listening" to your problems, as it were; yet you can feel completely free to write anything and everything you're thinking and feeling—
no one else will ever see the journal if you don't wish it. Keeping a journal
can also be very helpful in enabling you to judge how far you've come—to
record the successes in your life and the growth in yourself.

RECOMMENDED READING

THE BUSINESS OF ACTING

Buzzell, Linda. *How to Make It in Hollywood.* HarperCollins, 1992.

Callan, K. *How to Sell Yourself as an Actor.* Sweden Press, 1988.

Henry, Mari Lyn, and Lynne Rogers. *How to Be a Working Actor.* Back Stage Books, 1994.

Litwak, Mark. *Reel Power.* William Morrow, 1986.

Small, Edgar. *From Agent to Actor.* Samuel French, 1991.

Steel, Dawn. *They Can Kill You But They Can't Eat You.* Simon & Schuster, 1993.

CHILDHOOD

Bradshaw, John. *Bradshaw on the Family.* Health Communications, 1988.

_____. *Healing the Shame That Binds You.* Health Communications, 1988.

_____. *Homecoming.* Bantam Books, 1990.

Forward, Susan. *Toxic Parents.* Bantam Books, 1989.

Miller, Alice. *The Drama of the Gifted Child.* Basic Books, 1994.

_____. *For Your Own Good.* Noonday Press, 1990.

_____. *Thou Shalt Not Be Aware.* New American Library, 1986.

Missildine, W. Hugh. *Your Inner Child of the Past.* Simon & Schuster, 1963.

Stark, Amy. *Because I Said So.* Pharos Books, 1992.

SELF-ESTEEM, FULFILLMENT, SPIRITUALITY

Armstrong, Thomas. *Seven Kinds of Smart*. Plume, 1993.

Borysenko, Joan. *Fire in the Soul*. Warner Books, 1993.

_____. *Guilt Is the Teacher, Love Is the Lesson*. Warner Books, 1990.

Bramson, Robert M. *Coping with Difficult People*. Anchor Doubleday, 1981.

Buber, Martin. *I and Thou*. Collier/Macmillan, 1958.

Cameron, Julia. *The Artist's Way*. Putnam, 1992.

Gallwey, Timothy. *The Inner Game of Tennis*. Bantam Books, 1974.

Goldberg, Natalie. *Writing Down the Bones*. Shambhala Publications, 1986.

James, Jennifer. *Women and the Blues*. Harper & Row, 1988.

James, Muriel, and John James. *Passion for Life*. Dutton, 1991.

Kabat-Zinn, Jon. *Wherever You Go, There You Are*. Hyperion, 1994.

Kopp, Sheldon. *All God's Children Are Lost, But Only a Few Can Play the Piano*. Prentice Hall, 1991.

Langer, Ellen J. *Mindfulness*. Addison-Wesley, 1989.

Lehmkul, Dorothy, and Dolores Cotter Lamping. *Organizing for the Creative Person*. Crown, 1993.

Maisel, Eric. *Staying Sane in the Arts*. Putnam, 1992.

Moore, Thomas. *Care of the Soul*. HarperCollins, 1992.

Proto, Louis. *Take Charge of Your Life*. Thorsons Publishers, 1988.

Sher, Barbara. *I Could Do Anything If I Only Knew What It Was*. Delacorte Press, 1994.

Storr, Anthony. *Solitude: A Return to the Self*. Free Press, 1988.

Ueland, Brenda. *If You Want to Write: A Book About Art, Independence, and Spirit*. Graywolf Press, 1987.

Young, Jeffrey E., and Janet S. Klosko. *Reinventing Your Life*. Penguin, 1993.

MONEY

Chopra, Deepak. *Creating Affluence*. New World Library, 1993.

Dominguez, Joe, and Vicki Robin. *Your Money or Your Life*. Viking Penguin, 1992.

Laut, Phil. *Money Is My Friend*. Ballantine Books, 1979.

Lieberman, Annette, and Vicki Lindner. *Unbalanced Accounts: How Women Can Overcome Their Fear of Money*. Viking Penguin, 1987.

Sinetar, Marsha. *Do What You Love, the Money Will Follow*. Dell, 1987.

Winter, Barbara J. *Making a Living Without a Job*. Bantam Books, 1993.

INDEX